PUB WALKS

IN

Oxfordshire

THIRTY CIRCULAR WALKS
AROUND OXFORDSHIRE INNS

Nick Channer

COUNTRYSIDE BOOKS
NEWBURY, BERKSHIRE

First Published 1994
© Nick Channer 1994

Revised and updated 1998

COUNTRYSIDE BOOKS
3 Catherine Road
Newbury, Berkshire

ISBN 1 85306 303 7

Designed by Mon Mohan
Cover illustration by Colin Doggett
Photographs by the author
Maps by Bob Carr

Produced through MRM Associates Ltd., Reading
Typeset by Paragon Typesetters, Queensferry, Clwyd
Printed by Woolnough Bookbinding Ltd., Irthlingborough

Contents

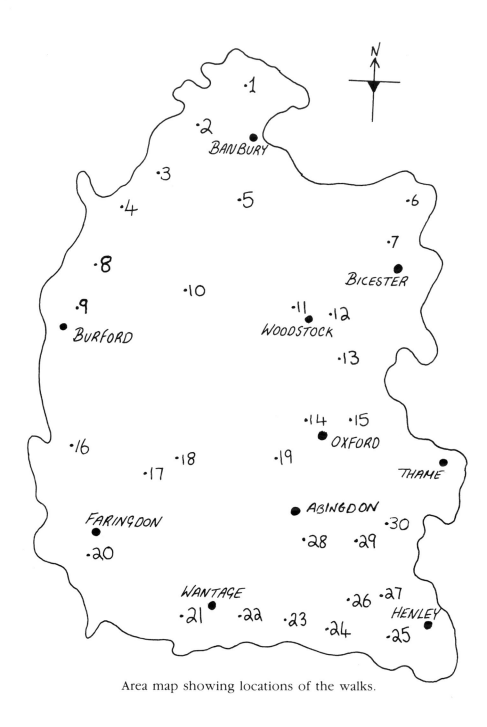

Area map showing locations of the walks.

Publisher's Note

We hope that you obtain considerable enjoyment from this book; great care has been taken in its preparation. However, changes of landlord and actual closures are sadly not uncommon. Likewise, although at the time of publication all routes followed public rights of way or well-established permitted paths, diversion orders can be made and permissions withdrawn.

We cannot accept responsibility for any inaccuracies, but we are anxious that all details covering both pubs and walks are kept up to date, and would therefore welcome information from readers which would be relevant to future editions.

Introduction

Oxfordshire is a county of contrasts. For the outdoor enthusiast and in particular the walker there is much to see and do. In the north and west of the county there are the eastern Cotswolds – that rich, rolling corner of Oxfordshire where picture-postcard cottages of honey-coloured stone seemingly have been preserved for all time. In the east are the glorious beechwoods of the Chilterns where, between the whispering trees, there are glimpses of distant rural landscapes. North-west of these hills lies Otmoor, a sinister tract of wetland expanse known as the 'loneliest place in the county'. The south-west corner of Oxfordshire includes the charming Vale of the White Horse, where there are stunning views over hills and dramatic downland ridges. Here, the timeless Ridgeway marches to distant horizons.

The rivers play an integral part too. The Cherwell, Evenlode and Windrush all flow through Oxfordshire – pretty names to reflect their gentle, unhurried nature. The majestic Thames is the county's main artery of water, flowing from west to east. And then there is the Oxford Canal, perhaps a lesser-known waterway but a delightful feature none the less. There are the villages too – Beckley, Shenington, Stratton Audley, Swinbrook, Great Tew, Kelmscott, Longworth and East Hendred among many others – all of them gems in the county's rural heartland.

Oxfordshire has more than its quota of fine houses and stately homes – what could possibly equal the scale and opulent splendour of Blenheim Palace? And, of course, at the very heart of the county is Oxford itself, likened by Thomas Hardy's Jude to 'the heavenly Jerusalem'. Its history, beauty and tradition are admired throughout the world.

To take advantage of the county's visual splendours, I have devised 30 walks which begin and end at a traditional inn and explore some of the best countryside in the south of England. In terms of both pubs and walks, I hope to have included something for everyone. Some of the inns are simple, straightforward and unpretentious, with a basic choice of standard bar meals. One or two are restaurant pubs with a stronger emphasis on good-quality food. Several are on the tourist trail and consequently can get very busy.

Each chapter contains a general account of the featured pub, including a representation of the menu, details of real ales and other information, including how to find the inn. Most of the pubs are open at the standard times. All welcome walkers, many permit children and dogs. Almost all have a car park where you can leave a vehicle whilst doing the walk; it is generally easier to complete the circuit before visiting the pub!

The walks accompanying the inns are all circular routes; anyone used to modest distances should not find these a problem. None is more than 5½ miles in length. Several routes follow stretches of long-distance paths, including the Oxfordshire Way, a 65-mile walk linking the Cotswolds and the Chilterns. As a safeguard, I would advise you to carry a copy of the relevant OS map, as well as a small rucksack containing such items as waterproof clothing and a camera.

Finally, I hope the walks reflect the distinctive character of Oxfordshire, its quiet beauty and its individual appeal. Enjoy them as they are meant to be enjoyed. And enjoy the pubs!

Nick Channer

1 Cropredy
The Brasenose Arms

The name Cropredy is thought to come from Old English – 'redy', meaning brook. This is a popular village on the banks of the Oxford Canal and the river Cherwell. In summer it comes alive with tourists and boating enthusiasts. In winter it is perfect for a quiet stroll beside the canal or in the surrounding countryside. The inn is a listed building situated on land owned by Brasenose College, Oxford – hence the name. In summer it is particularly popular with walkers and members of the boating fraternity. Inside there is the locals' bar and adjacent to it a small lounge bar and adjoining restaurant. Here there are prints of New Orleans and Canadian scenes; the emphasis on this side is more on food than drink.

Food is available every day, though not at lunchtime on Monday between September and March. Prawn cocktail and home-made soup are among the starters; main courses range from sirloin steak and cod to 8 oz pork chop and seaman's platter. Vegetarian meals include mushroom stroganoff and vegetable Mexicana. There are smaller portions of many dishes for children, a range of puddings and a selection of lighter snacks, including various home-filled sandwiches, ploughman's, jacket potatoes, jumbo sausage and several locally produced beef burgers. On Sunday there is usually a roast.

Real ales include Fuller's London Pride and Morland Old Speckled Hen; also on offer are Guinness, Carling, Kronenbourg and Strongbow cider. There is a choice of quality wines by the glass and bottle.

It is necessary to book the restaurant in advance; larger groups are also asked to telephone first. Children and well-behaved dogs are welcome. Outside is a beer garden with a play area for children. Telephone: 01295 750244.

How to get there: Cropredy is about 4 miles north of Banbury, just off the A423. The inn is on the left as you come into the village centre.

Parking: There is a car park at the side of the inn, and Cropredy has places suitable for parking.

Length of the walk: 3 miles. Map: OS Landranger 151 Stratford-upon-Avon and surrounding area (GR 467465).

The walk makes for Williamscot, passing the entrance to the main house, where Charles I is reputed to have stayed during a battle in the Civil War, and then returns to Cropredy along the canal towpath. Lines of narrow boats add a touch of colour to this pleasant walk, which will appeal to those interested in the great canal era. On the final straight of the walk you can pick out the church tower at Cropredy, overlooking the Cherwell valley.

The Walk

From the inn turn left and walk along the road for a short distance. Turn right at the green (by the letter-box), pass Church Lane, then bear right at the Methodist chapel. After a few yards cross into Red Lion Street and follow it down to the bend. At this point go straight on towards Prescote. Once over the Oxford Canal join the towpath and head south, immediately passing under the brick bridge. Pass a pretty cottage on the left and continue along to the next bridge where you leave the towpath and head for the road.

Bear left and walk towards Williamscot, crossing the bridge over the Cherwell. This is the site of a bloody battle in the Civil War. Parliamentary forces stormed the bridge but were pushed back by Royalist troops. According to some records, the people of Cropredy, fearing for the church and its possessions in the midst of battle, quickly seized an exquisite eagle lectern and plunged it into the river. However, they later forgot where exactly they had thrown it and many years passed before it was finally recovered and returned to the church.

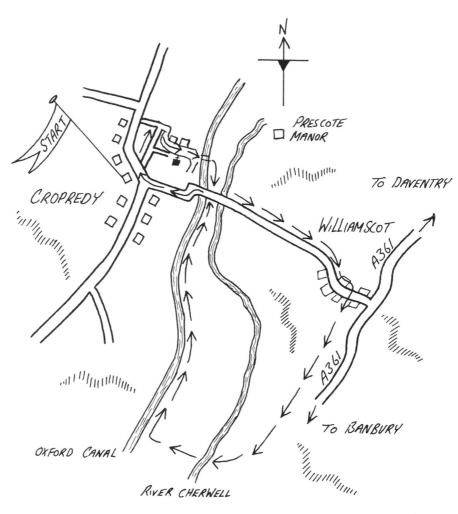

Continue along the road and note the sports field on the right. Follow the road between hedgerows, trees and fields; on the left are delightful, far-reaching views towards the Warwickshire border. Pass a lodge and a private drive and continue along the road. Soon you enter the village of Williamscot. Pass some pretty cottages on the right and then bear right by some bungalows. Walk down the lane towards the telephone box and pass Cannons Yard on the left. When the lane bends left continue ahead towards some farm buildings. Go over a stile and through several gates to follow a track heading away from the farm and down towards the Cherwell valley. There is a paddock on the left and sloping fields away to the right. The views at this point are spectacular; in the distance the Cherwell and the Oxford Canal can be seen cutting through the countryside.

Follow the field boundary down to a gate; the main road is visible over to the left. Keep on the track as it goes across the field and when it swings left towards the road, bear right to join a clear bridle-path. Go through the gate into the next field and continue towards power lines. Aim for the footbridge over the Cherwell and in the distance are the buildings of Pewet Farm. Cross the footbridge and then swing half-left to a stile in the next boundary. Join the canal towpath by the lock and bear right. Follow the towpath, pass under the bridge and continue towards Cropredy. Over to the right, between the trees, is the outline of Williamscot.

Make for the next bridge and then go on to the old run-down mill, seen on the opposite bank. Near it is Bourton House. Lines of moored narrow boats can be seen at this stage of the walk. The church tower at Cropredy edges into view now. Pass a British Waterways sign – please remember 4 mph speed limit!

On reaching the road bridge at Cropredy Wharf, leave the towpath, turn left and follow the road to the junction where the inn will be seen in front of you.

2 Shenington
The Bell

The picturesque village of Shenington possesses a splendid green and houses of mellow stone. The church has an impressive Tudor tower.

The Bell, overlooking the pretty village green, was built as an inn in the early part of the 18th century, making it nearly 300 years old. With the emphasis very much on food and a choice of Boddingtons, Hook Norton, Heineken, Guinness and Strongbow Dry Cider, this is an ideal inn to make for after an invigorating walk in the surrounding countryside.

There is a cosy log fire in the lounge bar, as well as a stone floor, horse brasses and plenty of beams. Adjoining the lounge is an intimate little family room and beyond that is the pine-panelled public bar which includes a dartboard. The menu is varied and appetising. Among the starters are home-made parsnip soup, kipper pâté and toast and prawn mousse and toast. Main dishes include steak and kidney pie; veal in ginger wine and cream; braised beef and vegetables; pork chop; plaice in Stilton sauce; almond, cashew and cherry bake; and chilli con carne. There is also a traditional Sunday roast. Food is available every day. There is also accommodation at this charming stone-built inn, and children and dogs are welcome.

Telephone: 01295 670274.

How to get there: From Banbury follow the A422 towards Stratford. Beyond Wroxton bear left (signposted Shenington). The inn is on the right when you reach the green.

Parking: There is room to park at the front of the inn, or elsewhere in the village.

Length of the walk: 3 ¾ miles. Map: Map: OS Landranger 151 Stratford-upon-Avon and surrounding area (GR 371428).

This walk traverses the rolling hills and undulating Cotswold landscape of north-west Oxfordshire. The route coincides for a time with the d'Arcy Dalton Way, a long-distance footpath of over 60 miles and established in 1985 to mark the golden jubilee of the Ramblers' Association. The way is named after the late Colonel W.P. d'Arcy Dalton who, for over 50 years, championed the need to preserve rights of way in Oxfordshire. Near the end the walk reaches the little church at Alkerton. Half hidden amid the trees, it occupies an idyllic setting.

The Walk

From the inn turn right towards the village green, then right at the junction and along Shenington's main street. Pass between lines of cottages; note Mill Lane and a development of houses called The Level. Continue through the village and when you reach the last bungalow on the left, veer half-left on to the d'Arcy Dalton Way. Descend the slopes of the field and in the bottom left corner use the footbridge to cross the little stream.

Head up the slopes; glancing back at this point allows you a memorable view of Shenington and the rolling farmland of north Oxfordshire. In the top left-hand corner of the field, go through a gate and along the left boundary of the field. In the next corner go through another gate and down the slope to another gate. Still following the route of the d'Arcy Dalton Way, go into the next field and follow the path diagonally left. There is a pond on the left. Cross over several stiles, go over a little footbridge and then cross another stile after a few yards, under some trees.

Veer diagonally right across the field, aiming for the top right corner. Look out here for the smooth, rounded summit of Epwell Hill, rising over 700 ft above sea level. A mile or so to the west of the walk is the Warwickshire border and beyond that is the stately Tudor mansion of Compton Wynyates. Regarded as one of the most visually striking houses in England, Compton Wynyates lies in a fold of the hills and was besieged and captured during the Civil War.

In the field corner go out to the road and bear left. Pass Epwell electricity substation. When you reach a junction – Epwell is

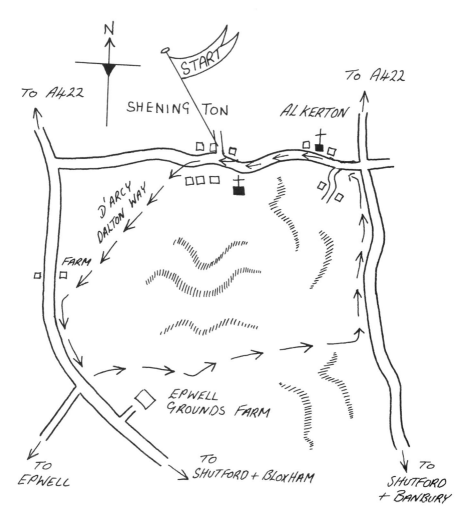

signposted right – turn left and go through a gate by an oak tree. Follow a bridleway towards the far field boundary and as you approach a barn veer right to a gate in the hedge. Go through it, then another gate with a sign requesting dogs to be kept on leads. Veer diagonally left across the field to join a clear track at the corner of a hedge. Follow the track with the hedge on your immediate right. Some barns are visible up ahead. If you glance back at this stage you will see the grassy mounds of Epwell Hill and Orchard Hill. When, after several minutes, you reach a gateway, swing left towards the

14

barns. Veer to the right by the buildings and look for a waymarker post up ahead.

Head out across the middle of a large field and look out over a vast, undulating rural landscape. Make for the gateway in the boundary up ahead. In the next field go slightly left and down the slope. Follow the vague outline of the path and pass beneath some pylons. Look for a gate and waymarker post in the trees and hedgerow. Cross a footbridge and then look for a gate in the next boundary. Go through the wooden gate, cross a dashing stream and then go up the bank. Swing left after a few yards to join a clear track running up the hillside. There is a hedge on the right. From the higher ground there are superb views over hills and wooded vales virtually as far as the eye can see.

At the road turn left towards Shenington. Follow the lane across the top of the hills towards a large farm. On reaching the next junction bear left and descend between trees and hedges into the village of Alkerton. Further down there is a sharp left turning (Well Lane). Opposite the turning is the entrance to the historic parish church of St Michael. The church dates back to the early 13th century. Inside are some carvings which are believed to depict the life and times of Edward the Black Prince, who was born at Woodstock in 1330. The church, which includes some massive Norman arches, is beautifully situated amid the trees and slopes. The adjacent rectory is Jacobean.

At the road turn right and walk up the hill to the green at Shenington. The inn is on the right.

3 Hook Norton
The Pear Tree Inn

The Pear Tree has been a brewery house since 1869, 20 years after a young man by the name of John Harris set up in business as a maltster supplying small brew houses in the area. Eventually this modest but enterprising venture led to the founding of the famous Hook Norton brewery, whose premises are just a stone's throw from the inn. Prints by a local artist and other publications on the brewery can be purchased from the pub.

The Pear Tree is a popular pub with a friendly atmosphere. Inside, there are low ceilings, beams, horse brasses and a panelled bar. Not surprisingly, Hook Norton is the chief brew among the real ales – there is Best Mild, Old Hooky and Best Bitter. The inn also provides bottled cider, and Carlsberg and Lowenbrau lagers. Bar food includes a range of traditional sandwiches, baked potatoes filled with cheese, prawn, tuna, beans and sausage; various ploughman's and soup. Main meals consist of Hooky casserole, haddock casserole, Thai chicken curry, home-made cottage pie, beef lasagne and home-cooked ham and eggs. There is also a selection of desserts, including pecan pie, rice pudding and hot lemon meringue, and there are various specials. No food is provided on Sunday night or Tuesday night. Bed and breakfast

accommodation is also available. Children and well-behaved dogs are welcome and there is a beer garden.
    Telephone: 01608 737482.

How to get there: Take the A361 between Banbury and Chipping Norton. The turning to Hook Norton is just to the east of Chipping Norton. As you come into the village, the inn will be seen on the left by the turning to Sibford Gower.

Parking: There is room to park at the inn, or in Hook Norton village.

Length of the walk: 5 miles. Map: OS Landranger 151 Stratford-upon-Avon and surrounding area (GR 351333).

In an age when many public houses are part of giant brewery chains, it is refreshing to learn of a small, old established family brewery producing fine traditional ales. Hook Norton brewery is one such place. The walk begins by taking you up the lane at the side of the inn to view the distinctive design of the building. After that it heads for the centre of Hook Norton, a sizeable ironstone village – in fact, the parish is one of the largest in the county. Details of a popular village trail can be purchased at the inn. The route is then across the striking hill country of north-west Oxfordshire, close to where it meets Warwickshire. To the south the walk runs along the edge of Swerford Park, once a ducal hunting lodge. The village of Swerford is one of the prettiest in the area.

The Walk

On leaving the inn turn left and then left again (Brewery Lane). The splendid Victorian façade of Hook Norton Brewery soon comes into view. There is a shop here but the Brewery itself is not open to the public. Return to the inn and at the junction bear left towards the centre of Hook Norton. Follow the lane between lines of cottages and houses and soon you pass the Baptist church and the parish church. Just before the Bell Inn turn right (signposted Swerford). This is Bell Hill. At the bottom, immediately beyond the bridge, turn left into Park Road.

    At the next junction continue ahead with a row of bungalows on the left. When the road bends left join a signposted bridleway. Follow the track towards the remains of the old railway viaduct on the now disused Banbury to Cheltenham line. Seven stone pillars serve as a sad reminder of the golden days of the railways, a monument to the great era of steam travel.

    On reaching a cattle grid and a gate, just beyond the buildings of

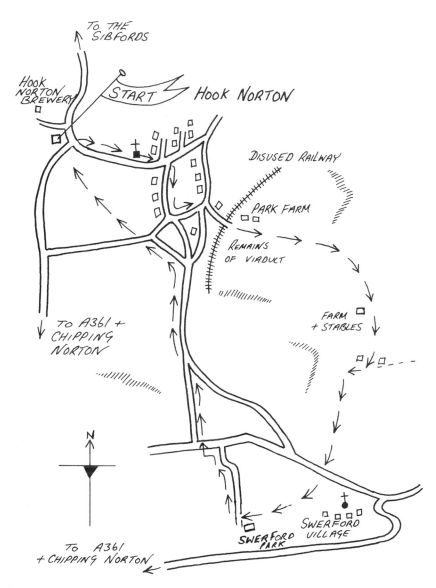

Park Farm, veer slightly left towards another gate by some trees. Continue along the bridleway; there are good views on the right over rolling, well-wooded countryside. Continue along the track when you reach the next gate. Avoid a waymarked path on the left as the track curves right. Go through another gate and then you reach a ford.

18

There is a footbridge here. Pass through yet another gate and then follow the track along a field boundary. Go through another gate and continue across the fields towards a house up on the hill. Beyond another gate follow the field edge and in the corner go through a gate and then turn immediately right to the next gate. Go slightly right, aiming for a waymark, then turn right to reach a gate. Turn left and walk along the main drive.

Cut through a landscape of fields, trees and hedgerows; in the distance you can just spot traffic on the main A361 road. Eventually you reach some barns; at a sign for Cradle Farm bear right and leave the drive. Follow a muddy bridleway; on the right is a pair of semi-detached houses, and after a few yards the bridleway curves to the left and ascends the hill. The church spire at Swerford is visible a little to the left down amongst the trees in the charming valley of the Swere. Follow the track to the road and then go straight across and continue on the bridleway. Soon the track becomes a vague grassy outline; there is a fence and some trees on the left. The delightful village of Swerford can easily be seen along this stretch.

In the field corner go through a gate and then bear right to enter the next field. Continue in the same direction as before with the field boundary on your left. Cross into the next field via a gate and then pass to the right of some fencing when you reach the grounds of Swerford Park. On reaching a tree-lined drive turn right and follow it to the road. Bear left and soon you reach a turning on the right to Hook Norton. Take the lane and follow it between trees and hedgerows.

Soon the road descends gently and now the houses of Hook Norton come into view down below. The church stands out proudly amidst the buildings. The remains of the old viaduct are also visible now. When you reach the 30 mph speed limit sign, with some picturesque cottages in front of you, bear left and pass the Pound House. The road twists and turns through the village of Hook Norton. At the end of a line of bungalows on the right, cross a stile and follow a pleasant field path towards some trees in the dip. The church is a short distance away on the right. Down in the field corner, beside a pretty stream which meanders through the fields, go over several stiles and then continue along the right-hand edge of the next field. The stream is on the right, enclosed by a belt of trees. Go down to a stile beside some cottages and out to the road. Turn right and then left and return to the inn.

4 Chipping Norton
The Blue Boar

Chipping Norton, or 'Chippy' as the locals call it, prospered as a result of the wool trade and is one of the gateways to the Cotswolds. It is the highest town in Oxfordshire and boasts a fine wide market place. The church, though not prominently situated in the town, is impressive.

The popular rambling old Blue Boar inn lies at the heart of Chipping Norton, offering views of the market place and the town's many historic buildings. A stone inside the inn indicates that the building dates back to the late 17th century; the restaurant is understood to have been the stables originally. For a number of years the Blue Boar was a commercial hotel; one or two black and white photographs bear this out. Several breweries owned it – according to one of the locals, whose grandfather is pictured in one of the old photographs, Hunt Edmunds acquired it from Chipping Norton brewery in the 1920s and then Flowers owned it in more recent years. It is now a freehouse.

The large stone-walled main bar is semi-divided with arches and pillars; there is also a stone-flagged conservatory or garden room and an adjacent restaurant. The Blue Boar is a place for real ale enthusiasts and the choice of beers changes frequently. It also provides Guinness,

Foster's Kronenbourg 1664 and Dry Blackthorn cider. The bar menu offers a good choice of food – home-made steak and kidney pie, deep-fried scampi, sausage, egg, chips and beans, grilled gammon steak, various filled baguettes and vegetarian stir-fry are among the popular dishes. The culinary picture is completed by jacket potatoes, omelettes and salads, home-made soup, ploughman's, country pâté, a range of sandwiches, including prawn, ham and cheese and pickle, a children's menu and a choice of desserts – ice-cream and sorbets among them. The restaurant menu is popular and varied. It is advisable to book in advance if you want to eat in the restaurant on Friday, Saturday or Sunday. Large parties also would do well to book beforehand. The Blue Boar serves food every day and is open all day from Monday to Saturday, and from 12 noon to 10.30 pm on Sunday. Well-behaved dogs are permitted inside. There is no beer garden.
Telephone: 01608 643525.

How to get there: Follow the A44 between Oxford and Stratford and then follow the signs to Chipping Norton. The inn is at the northern end of the market place.

Parking: There is no car park at the Blue Boar. However, a free car park is available just off the A44. From the market place follow the road round the corner, towards Moreton-in-Marsh. After a few yards you will see a turning on the left to the car park and squash club.

Length of the walk: 3 miles. Map: OS Landranger 164 Oxford and surrounding area (GR 314273).

The walk offers memorable views over the Cotswolds. From Chipping Norton it heads for the neighbouring village of Over Norton and the parkland of Over Norton House before returning to the town.

The Walk
From the front of the inn walk ahead through the market place and then bear right to follow the A44 down the hill. Pass Penhurst School on the right and then enter the recreation ground. Follow the sign for Salford and pass the adventure playground. On the left you may catch a glimpse of Chipping Norton's famous Victorian Bliss Valley Tweed Mill. Go through a kissing-gate and down the slope to a footbridge in the dip. Cross it and then make for some houses up on the hillside. Aim for several stiles to the left of them – there is a drive lined by trees between the stiles. Once over the stiles follow the right-hand boundary of the field to its top corner.

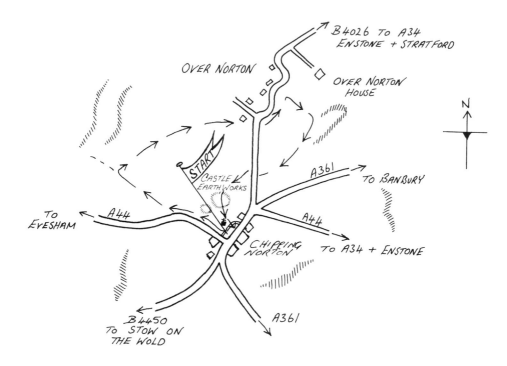

In the next field continue to follow the right-hand edge; in the corner bear left and then after a few yards turn right through the gap in the hedge. Follow the field boundary with a copse on your right. Ahead of you is a spectacular scene as you look over the rolling fields of north-west Oxfordshire. The village of Salford can be glimpsed in the distance. At the end of the trees follow the track as it bends sharp right, heading for the village of Over Norton. Pass a turning on the right and continue.

Further on there is a glorious wide panorama from the higher ground. To the west the view is predominantly of the Cotswolds – that delightful region of the country so perfectly typified by soft green hills, wooded vales, and ancient exquisite towns of mellow, honey-coloured stone. Pass the turning to a corrugated barn and transmitter on the left.

Follow the track towards the houses of Over Norton. On the right is a drystone wall enclosing several properties set amidst the trees. At the road junction (Cleeves Corner) veer left along the main street of Over Norton. Note a turning on the right to Little Rollright and continue along the village street towards Great Rollright.

22

When you reach a bus shelter on the right, veer right and follow the waymarked path between houses. Pass to the left of a timber chalet, go through a gate and into a field. Go down the grassy slope towards some woodland. Pass through a gate into the trees and continue straight ahead on a clear path. Soon you reach a cottage on the left. At this point turn right on to a waymarked path, cross over a ditch and follow a clear path through rough grass and between trees. Go over a ladder stile and continue through the parkland of Over Norton House.

Keep the strip of woodland on your right and walk ahead. Where the ground may be wet and boggy, move to the higher ground for a brief spell and then return to the route of the walk. Look for a stile ahead in the next fence. Pass into the next field and press on towards a clump of trees. Emerge from the parkland beside several stone pillars and at the road turn right. Follow the road between lines of trees, go over a stone bridge and then cross over to a kissing-gate about 100 yards before the Over Norton village sign. Follow the path, muddy in places, with woodland on the left. In the field corner go through another kissing-gate and follow the woodland path. A sparkling little stream runs alongside the path at this stage of the walk and then disappears from view into a drain beside you. The path runs through a tunnel before reaching some higher ground. On the right the wooded slopes run down into a picturesque dell.

Soon the path emerges from the trees; fields slope down to the right of you and in the distance there are glimpses of trees and hedgerows and maybe a horse grazing in a paddock. On the left the houses of Chipping Norton creep into view. The mighty tower of the parish church can now be seen up ahead. Go through another kissing-gate by the entrance to Cleeves Barn and walk up the drive and round to the right. At the junction you will see the church ahead and all around you are the remains of what was an imposing Norman castle. Turn left here and walk up to the next junction. Bear right into Market Street and return to the market place in the centre of Chipping Norton.

5 Great Tew
The Falkland Arms

Arthur Mee, in his book *The King's England – Oxfordshire*, says that 'if our England is a garden Great Tew is one of its rare plots'. Peacefully located on the slopes of a scenic, richly wooded valley and thankfully bypassed by busy roads, Great Tew is, without question, one of the most beautiful villages in Oxfordshire, a gem of a place that has to be seen to be fully appreciated. Originally designed as an estate village in the 19th century, with the intention of blending architectural beauty with utility and agricultural management, Great Tew went into decline in later years and virtually became derelict. Thankfully the village has been given a new lease of life, with many of the thatched and ironstone cottages painstakingly restored, and now Great Tew has been designated an Outstanding Conservation Area.

The Falkland Arms is one of the finest inns in Oxfordshire. A pub and hotel of great charm and character, it appears in countless guides on inns, food and drink. There has been an inn on this site for about 500 years; originally the name of the inn was the Horse and Groom but it was changed in the 19th century to commemorate the Falkland family who became owners of the manor. Inside, there is much to see: a cosy inglenook fireplace, oak panelling, flagstones, high-backed settles, an assortment of clay pipes and a huge collection of antique Doulton beer mugs and jugs hanging from the ceiling. Real ales include Wadworth 6X, Tanglefoot and Hook Norton Best Bitter – there is also a choice of four guest ales and a wide selection of traditional country wines, dry and medium sweet cider, and mulled wine in winter.

The menu comprises home-made dishes including steak and kidney pie, soup, beef and Stilton pie, chicken and leek pie, lamb shoulders, ploughman's, mushrooms in cider, several vegetarian meals, and a selection of puddings. In summer the menu also includes a range of salads, quiches and other light meals. Food is served every lunchtime between 12 noon and 2 pm and you can eat in the dining room every evening except Sunday, between 7 pm and 8 pm. Bookings are not taken for lunch but it is essential to make an evening reservation for the dining room. Outside is a front patio, with a charming beer garden at the rear. Sunday night is folk-music night and at this time the inn can get very busy. Bed and breakfast accommodation includes two rooms with four poster beds. Well-behaved dogs are permitted inside the pub, and children are allowed in the small dining room at lunchtime only.

Telephone: 01608 683653.

How to get there: From Oxford and Woodstock follow the A44 towards Chipping Norton. Turn right at Enstone and join the B4022. The turning to Great Tew is on the right. The Falkland Arms is in the village centre.

Parking: There is no car park at the inn. However, Great Tew has a free car park nearby.

Length of the walk: 2¾ miles. Map: OS Landranger 164 Oxford and surrounding area (GR 396293).

The walk visits the splendid church of St Michael, then circumnavigates Tew Park before culminating in a tour of the village itself.

The Walk
From the Falkland Arms turn right and then left by the primary school. At the junction turn left and go up the hill. Looking back, there are glorious views over the wooded parkland.

Pass the entrance to St Michael's church – a splendid avenue of laurels and traveller's joy leads you to this lovely old building which lies peacefully amid the trees of the parkland. The stone gateway was restored in 1992 and, according to the plaque, the church walk was formerly the carriage drive to the mansion of Lucius Carey, 2nd

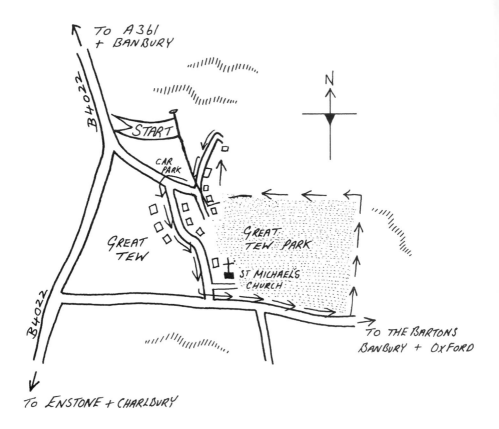

To A361 + BANBURY

B4022

START

CAR PARK

GREAT TEW

GREAT TEW PARK

ST MICHAELS CHURCH

N

To THE BARTONS BANBURY + OXFORD

B4022

To ENSTONE + CHARLBURY

Viscount Falkland. In the 17th century the manor was inherited by the Viscount, a renowned classical scholar, poet and generous host who moved among the most elite circles of the day. Falkland later became Secretary of State to Charles I but was killed in 1643, serving as an ordinary trooper in the First Battle of Newbury.

Follow the road to the junction, swing left and walk along the edge of the tree-lined lane. Pass a turning on the right signposted to Tracey and Beaconsfield farms only. Continue along the lane with the parkland boundary on the left. There are glimpses of the estate along this stretch. Continue along the lane and eventually you reach a waymarked path on the left (signposted to Nether Worton). Take the path and follow it alongside the parkland wall. To the right are glorious views over a wide area of rural Oxfordshire. Follow the path down into the field corner and then cross into the next field via the gap in the trees.

Continue ahead with the field boundary still on your left; go down into the bottom left-hand corner of the field and then pass into the next field; over to your right is Hobbshole Farm. The parkland, dotted with majestic cedar trees, is visible on the left beyond the dilapidated stone wall. In the next corner you come upon a junction of paths. Turn left and follow a clear track with the northern boundary of Tew Park on your left. Ahead of you and to the right are glorious views over rolling, well-wooded country. Drop down a gentle slope to the field corner; continue ahead along the track, go into the next field via a gate and now the houses of Great Tew become visible, dotted amidst the trees. Pass through another gate in the field corner and continue with an ivy-covered wall on your immediate left. On reaching a thatched cottage turn right and follow a path down to a paddock; descend the grassy slopes to a gate in front of a stone house. Cross a tumbling brook, bear sharp left and follow the path between hedgerows. Join a drive and follow it to a junction.

Bear left and follow the lane back to the centre of Great Tew, passing the family butcher's shop on the right. Further on is the village post office – note the sign 'Post Office for money order, savings bank, parcel post, telegraph'. The Falkland Arms is further on along the street, on the left.

6 Finmere
The Red Lion

This thatched inn is understood to predate the Civil War, in which this area of Oxfordshire played an important part. Originally the pub was known as the Squirrels (there is a house of the same name in the village), but the flag of Charles I was hung over the old inn sign to demonstrate allegiance to the King and the name of the Red Lion has remained ever since.

This is a popular pub where children are welcome. Inside, there is a cosy log fire, horse brasses and beams. Look out for various prints of the Red Lion, one of which depicts the inn in the snow.

Strongbow draught cider is available here, as is Fuller's and London Pride. Winter ales include Fuller's Honeysuckle. Chiswick Keg Bitter, Guinness, Carling Black Label and Stella Artois are also on offer.

The inn includes a selection of fine wines and the menu offers a good selection of freshly cut sandwiches and freshly prepared salads; there are also ploughman's, filled baguettes, jacket potatoes and a double jumbo sausage. Starters range from soup of the day and prawn cocktail to mushrooms in cheese and garlic sauce and fisherman's platter. Main meals include cottage pie, beef and basil lasagne, 16 oz steak, Guinness pie, cod and mackerel. Egg salad and Stilton and

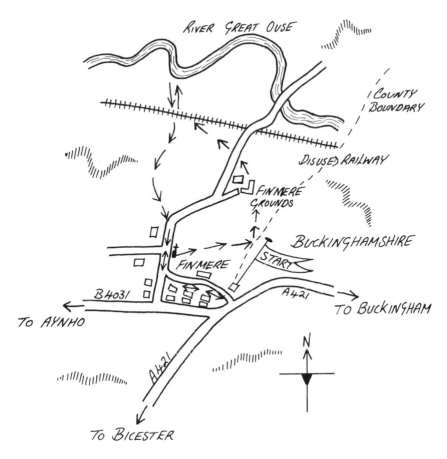

cauliflower are among the vegetarian dishes, and there is also lobster in batter and scampi.

Homemade specials include shepherds pie and chilli con carne; and puddings range from apple pie and treacle tart to ice cream and apple crumble. There is also a children's menu. The inn is open all day on Sunday when there is a traditional roast. Booking is preferred. No dogs please.

Telephone: 01280 847836.

How to get there: Finmere lies at the junction of the B4031 and A421 and is about 5 miles west of Buckingham. The inn is near the junction.

Parking: There is a car park at the side of the inn, and occasionally one or two parking spaces can be found in Finmere.

Length of the walk: 3¼ miles. Map: OS Landranger 165 Aylesbury and Leighton Buzzard area (GR 641327).

Finmere means 'a mere frequented by woodpeckers'. However, I did not see any when undertaking this pleasant walk which begins right on the Oxfordshire/ Buckinghamshire county boundary. From here the route goes through the village and then across country to the river Great Ouse. All around you are superb views over a wide rural landscape.

The Walk

Leave the inn and turn immediately right into Mere Road. Walk alongside various houses and cottages. Pass Town Close on the right and follow the road down to the junction with Valley Road. Bear right and pass Chinalls Close on the left. Veer right (signposted Water Stratford and Dadford). Turn immediately right and follow a stony track to the church gate. Enter the churchyard and then bear right to exit by a wooden kissing-gate. Cross a track and make for a gap ahead in the next boundary. Beyond it veer right for a few yards to pass alongside some farm buildings. Beyond them look for a gap in the right-hand hedge, taking you into the adjacent field. Follow a clear track between fence and hedgerow, still heading east. The buildings of Finmere are over to your right.

As you drop down the slope look for a wooden gate on the left. Pass through it and then follow the vague path over the high ground towards some farm buildings – this is Finmere Grounds Farm. Aim for the right-hand side of the buildings to reach the road. Cross it into the field and then veer half-right. The outline of the path is just visible. In the next field head diagonally towards the river valley and continue down to the gap in the right-hand boundary hedge.

Pass over the route of the disused Banbury-Buckingham branch line. Go through a gate and straight across the field towards a line of trees and a footbridge. On reaching the bridge it is worth pausing for a few moments to admire the pretty, rustic scene. The river Great Ouse flows through the peaceful countryside at this point.

Retrace your steps to the old railway line, then go straight on up the middle of a huge field; there is a vague grassy path along here. All around you are extensive views. Eventually you reach a gate in the field boundary, on a bend in the road. Head straight on and back towards Finmere. Pass the turning to Rosetthorpe, a private house. Return to the village centre, bear left into Mere Road and walk back to the inn.

Stratton Audley
The Red Lion

Near the church at Stratton Audley are the remains of a moated castle built by the Audleys. James Audley was one of the original Knights of the Garter, and the Black Prince gave him a pension for his efforts. There is strong evidence of the Roman invasion in this area. The nearby A421 is an old Roman road and the 'Stratton' in the village's name means enclosure on a Roman road.

Dating back to the 1400s and possibly connected to the church, the Red Lion is a picturesque thatched village inn. From the outside the pub looks quite small, but once inside you realise it is larger than it appears, and it includes a separate dining room and function room. There are some traditional pub features, such as low beams, stone walls and log fires. The inn places a strong emphasis on food and the choice of bar snacks includes a selection of sandwiches and jacket potatoes. For something more substantial you can choose from a wide menu. Starters may be soup of the day, potato wedges and garlic dip. Among the main dishes are steak and kidney pie, gammon steak, chicken curry, ham, egg and chips, sirloin steak and stir-fried Cajun chicken. Ploughman's and a choice of basket meals are also provided. On Sunday there is a roast at lunchtime, but no food in the evening.

Regular ales are served by Theakstons Best and Fullers London Pride, with the occasional guest ale. Stowford Press cider is also available. A popular pub with cyclists and ramblers, the Red Lion gets crowded at weekends, so it is advisable to book. Well-behaved children are welcome, but preferably no dogs.
Telephone: 01869 277225.

How to get there: Follow the A421 Bicester – Buckingham road towards Buckingham. The turning to Stratton Audley is on the right coming from the south. At the junction in the village centre turn right and the inn is on the left.

Parking: Though the inn has no car park there is plenty of room to park in the street outside.

Length of the walk: 2¾ miles. Map: OS Landranger 164 Oxford and surrounding area (GR 607263).

This is a pretty walk; initially it follows the Cross Bucks Way to the east of the village, then returns to Stratton Audley along field boundaries and woodland paths.

The Walk
On leaving the inn turn left and pass the entrance to Stratton Audley Manor. Walk round to the church on the right and just beyond it turn right (signposted Marsh Gibbon and Launton). Opposite the church bear left on to a waymarked path (Cross Bucks Way – Marsh Gibbon 3 miles). Walk across a paddock; on the left are views of Stratton Audley. In the next corner go straight on with a paddock and fence on your immediate left. One or two buildings are visible over to your right. In the next field corner, cross a stile, then another stile and a footbridge. Follow a grassy strip along the field edge – the hedge is on your left. Stratton Audley is still visible behind you, though the buildings of the village are now distantly glimpsed amid the trees. All around you are views over rolling farmland; away to the right there are glimpses of hills on the far horizon.

On the far side of the field cross a ditch, then a stile and now begin to veer half-left to another footbridge. Go into the next field and swing right to the tree-lined edge of the field. Keep to the edge of the field, following the vacillating line of the path. In the field corner bear left, leaving the route of the Cross Bucks Way; this waymarked path continues in an easterly direction towards the Buckinghamshire border and beyond. Follow the field edge, keeping the hedge on your

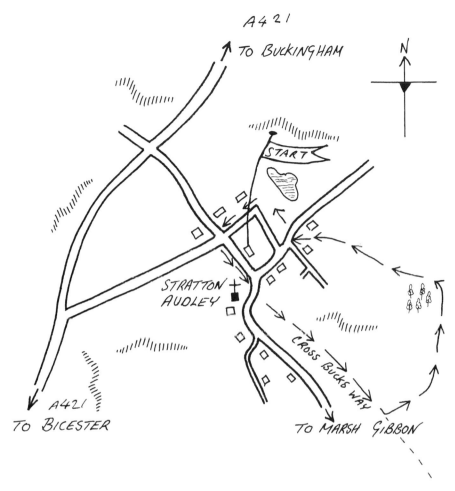

right. In the top corner go through the gap into the next field and keep to the right hand boundary. In the next corner follow the grassy path round to the left and then between two fields. There is a ditch on your right. Follow the track to the next corner where there is a plantation in front of you. The true line of the path is through the young trees but to make things a little easier, I would suggest you follow the boundary path round the side of the plantation, keeping the established woodland on your left. When you reach the end of the woodland on the left swing left into the next field via a wooden footbridge. Turn left and reach the field corner after a few yards. Pass through a wooden gate with the woodland on your left. In the next field corner go through another gate and join a wooded path alongside a stream. When you emerge from the trees, go straight across the field to a gate on the far side. Bear right in the adjacent field and follow the boundary towards a belt of woodland. On reaching the trees look for a gap where a gate takes you into the next field. Cross it to the gap in the next boundary and cross a stile and a footbridge. On the far side of the field go over another stile and footbridge and then veer slightly left across this elongated field. Look for a double stile half hidden in the hedgerow. Cross into the next field and then go diagonally left to the far wooded corner.

Cross a stile into a copse. Follow the path alongside some outbuildings and a cottage to the road. Cross over to a waymarked path and follow it along the edge of some trees. A lake comes into view now. Follow the path alongside the lake; there is a stone wall on the left. Bear left to the road junction. Go straight ahead into Cherry Street. At the next junction turn left and return to the inn.

⑧ Shipton-under-Wychwood
The Shaven Crown Hotel

The charmingly named Shipton-under-Wychwood is part of what remains of the ancient Forest of Wychwood. It is a lovely corner of the Cotswolds, and this delightful walk offers plenty of views over typical rolling hills and vales. Near the start it crosses the river Evenlode, described by Hilaire Belloc as 'a lovely river, all alone . . . forgotten in the western wolds'.

The Tourist Board lists the Shaven Crown as one of the ten oldest inns and hotels in the country. It certainly has a fascinating and well-documented history. Originally a late 14th century guest house or hospice for the monks of nearby Bruern Abbey, parts of it are also understood to have been used as a hunting lodge by Elizabeth I. It became an inn in 1571. The notorious fascist Oswald Mosley was imprisoned here during the last war. The family-owned Shaven Crown is a most attractive building of local honey-coloured stone and is very popular with visitors to the Cotswolds, who never fail to be impressed by its original 14th century gateway, medieval hall, with its double-collar braced roof, mullioned windows and central courtyard garden. Originally the stables, the beamed bar overlooks the garden and features a whimsical quotation:

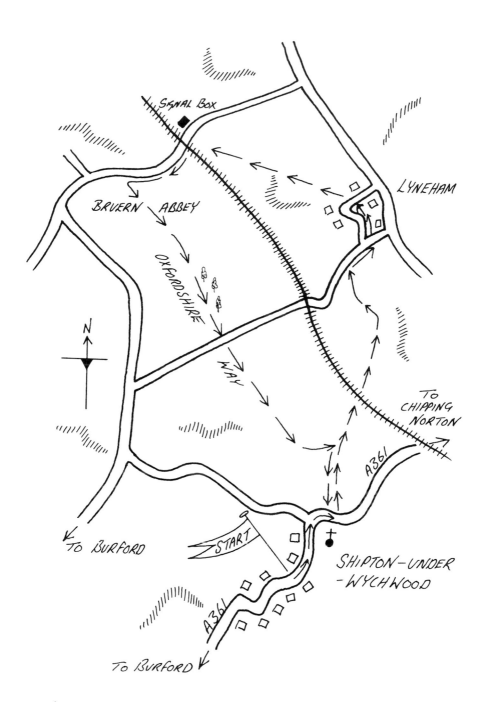

SIGNAL BOX

LYNEHAM

BRUERN ABBEY

OXFORDSHIRE

WAY

N

TO CHIPPING NORTON

A361

TO BURFORD

START

SHIPTON-UNDER-WYCHWOOD

A361

TO BURFORD

The reputation of a man is like his shadow, it sometimes follows or precedes him, it is sometimes longer and sometimes shorter than himself.

Real ales include Hook Norton Best Bitter; there are always two guest ales which changes frequently. Carlsberg, Guinness and a good selection of reasonably priced wines are also available. The bar menu includes game soup laced with sherry as a starter; main dishes vary from beef and mushroom pie cooked in ale to salmon fishcakes in rich tomato sauce. Vegetarian dishes and a range of sizzling platters also form part of the fare. There are also ploughman's, salads in summer and a range of specials and puddings. Children and dogs are welcome. The inn provides morning coffee and afternoon tea for non residents. Telephone: 01993 830330.

How to get there: Shipton-under-Wychwood lies on the A361, between Burford and Chipping Norton. The inn is on the left as you approach from Burford.

Parking: There is a car park at the Shaven Crown, and also some spaces in the village.

Length of the walk: 4½ miles. Map: OS Landranger 163 Cheltenham and Cirencester (GR 277177).

At one stage the walk coincides with the route of the d'Arcy Dalton Way (see Walk 2 for more information on this long-distance path). Halfway round the circuit you reach Bruern Abbey. The return leg of the walk follows a stretch of the Oxfordshire Way.

The Walk
At the road turn left and walk along the main road. Pass Bradleys Garage and follow the road round the sharp right-hand bend towards Chipping Norton and Banbury. After several minutes take the turning on the left (signposted Oxfordshire Way). Pass some houses on the left and then a new residential development of stone clad houses. Cross a footbridge and continue along the Oxfordshire Way between hedgerows. Soon you pass a turning on the left – this is the return leg of the walk.

Cross the stile and continue ahead along the right-hand edge of the field. In the corner go over the river Evenlode and head for the railway tunnel. Once through the tunnel swing left and make for a footbridge in the distant boundary. In the next field veer diagonally right to the boundary and then follow it down to the corner where you go through a gate. After a few yards you swing half-right across the field, beside signs of Anglo-Saxon strip farming, to its right-hand corner and then exit through a gate to the road.

Turn right and walk along the lane to the next junction. Bear left towards the buildings of Lyneham, a peaceful hamlet. Stone cottages, sympathetic barn conversions and trim gardens make up the scene here. When the road bears right go straight on along a stony track. Follow it past a golf course and at a pair of cottages and a gate swing left for a few yards and then veer half-right across the fairways and between the greens of the golf course. Aim for some cottages and a railway crossing in the distance.

Eventually you come down to the corner of the course; go over a footbridge, cross a stile and emerge at the road at Bruern crossing. The old signal box is visible on the right – a nostalgic reminder of the great railway days of old.

Turn left and cross the Oxford – Worcester railway (the Cotswold Line), then the river Evenlode. Carry on along the lane, between fields, trees and meadows. The extensive grounds of the present Bruern Abbey, enclosed by high yew hedges, are on the left at this point. The present building, which soon comes into view, is early 18th century. There was a Cistercian Abbey here around the middle of the 12th century. The present house was the home of Sir John Cope, who was commander in chief of the forces in Scotland at the time of the rebellion of 1745. Various striking houses and cottages can be seen at the side of the road.

Continue along the road until you reach the route of the Oxfordshire Way. Turn left into the parkland of Bruern Abbey and then aim half-left. The elegant façade of Bruern Abbey is visible over to the left. Follow the signs for the Oxfordshire Way and pass between the trees of the parkland. Enter a field and walk straight ahead along a strip of turf towards Bruern Wood. On reaching the trees you join a grassy ride. At the end of the ride, look for a gap in the left-hand corner, go through a wooden gate and out to a field edge.

Walk ahead across the open field, keeping to its right-hand edge. A pleasant rural landscape unfolds before you. Follow the path as it becomes enclosed by fencing. Cross a lane and continue along the path. The standard of waymarking is excellent on this stretch of the walk – so it is not easy to get lost! Continue across several fields and then bear left at a boundary hedge. Follow the path down to the field corner and then link up with the initial section of the walk. Turn right and retrace your steps back to the pub.

9 Swinbrook
The Swan

This lovely old building dates back 400 years and has long been associated with the adjoining mill, possibly providing accommodation for it. It is not a family pub – children and dogs are not permitted and there is no beer garden. However, walkers are welcome and the wide ranging menu is appetising, with an abundance of good-quality dishes. Inside, there are antique furnishings, flagstones and various artefacts. It is rumoured that the inn is haunted, but the landlord would not be drawn!

Speckled Hen is among the real ales, with Stowford Press draught cider also available. Unusually, there is also vintage dry cider from the cellar. The Swan has increased its menu in recent years to suit all tastes and as well as a variety of fish dishes, including haddock and cod, there are various ploughman's, toasted sandwiches and a selection of puddings, including apple crumble and chocolate fudge cake. Most Sundays there is a traditional roast. No food is provided on Sunday night. Being on the edge of the Cotswolds, and very close to the pretty river Windrush, the inn gets busy with tourists on summer weekends and bank holidays.

Telephone: 01993 822165.

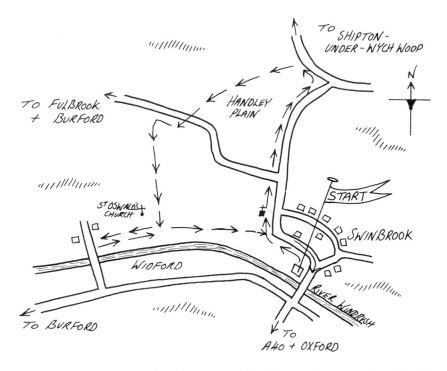

How to get there: Swinbrook is several miles to the east of Burford. Take the A40 towards Oxford and then turn left for Swinbrook. The inn is on the left just beyond a crossroads and the river Windrush.

Parking: There is limited parking at the inn and in Swinbrook.

Length of the walk: 3 miles. Map: OS Landranger 163 Cheltenham and Cirencester (GR 283118).

In summer Swinbrook is alive with tourists and walkers; in winter it is quiet and peaceful. Whatever the season, the setting in the valley of the Windrush is idyllic. The walk follows a quiet country lane for a while, then crosses Handley Plain to reach the little church of St Oswald at Widford. After a stroll round the hamlet return to Swinbrook by following the path across the meadows.

The Walk
On leaving the inn turn left and walk towards Swinbrook village centre. Disregard the turning on the right and follow the sign for the Oxfordshire Cycle Way. Follow the lane as it runs in a northerly direction out of the village, keeping to the left of a red telephone box.

The church, which is on the left, includes various family monuments and effigies dedicated to the Fettiplace family. They lived locally and it is claimed that at one time they held land in as many as 15 other counties. Their home at Swinbrook has now gone, but after they left it was taken over by a highwayman who robbed the upper ranks of local society.

Continue along the lane with a ditch on the right and a stone wall on the left. Rolling fields provide the scene here. Pass lines of cottages and a turning on the left to Fulbrook. The lane continues between cottages and stone walls, hedges and trees. On the higher ground you can see the river Windrush meandering through the valley below. Follow the lane round to the left towards some more cottages. The road is signposted to Shipton-under-Wychwood. When the road bends right swing left to join a no through road, with a duck-pond on the right.

Follow the narrow, single-track lane for a few yards. When it swings right continue ahead up a steepish, muddy track between stone walls. Go through a gate and continue along the bridleway. As you head across Handley Plain, there are good views over this undulating Cotswold country. Further on, the track cuts between high hedges to reach the road.

Turn right and follow the road. There are trees and hedgerow on the left and open fields on the right. The road descends a slope and further down is a gap in the left-hand boundary wall. The path here is signposted to Swinbrook and Widford. A sign refers to ground-nesting birds and the need to keep dogs under control.

Follow the path down towards Widford. This is a particularly striking stretch of the route, as the walk cuts between bursts of woodland and on down to the pretty meadows of the Windrush. At the next boundary go straight ahead towards a cottage. On the right at this point you can see the little medieval church of St Oswald, built on the site of a Roman villa. Remains of a mosaic floor can be seen near the altar.

Turn right and follow the path across the fields to the road. Bear left and walk along as far as the bridge over the Windrush. Retrace your steps to the church and then continue ahead towards Swinbrook. Enter the next field and begin to approach the village. The Windrush can be seen winding through the attractive countryside.

Cross a stile and veer a little to the right towards the houses and cottages of Swinbrook. Go through a gate and follow a path between stone walls and cottages. At the road turn right and return to the inn.

10 Finstock
The Plough

Originally just a forest clearing, Finstock has grown in size over the years. T.S. Eliot, raised as a Unitarian in the USA, was baptized in the Victorian church after becoming a British citizen in 1927.

As well as being a delightful pub with low-beamed ceilings and a thatched roof, the Plough is also an ideal venue for a romantic weekend touring the Cotswolds – at the rear of the building is a double room with a four-poster bed!

Inside the Plough, which is late 18th century, is the main lounge bar, dining area and flagstoned public bar. There are several black and white photographs of the inn and one or two prints of local rural scenes. Real ales include Hook Norton Best Bitter, Adnams Broadside and a guest ale. Merrydown cider is also available, as is Flowers bitter, Murphy's stout and Heineken and Stella Artois lager. In summer there is authentic cider from the barrel. The food is good and includes a choice of specials. Starters, which also adapt very well to light snacks, include pâté, garlic mushrooms, king prawns and home-made soup. Main courses range from steak and fish of the day to vegetarian crêpes and steak and kidney pie. Bar snacks include Oxfordshire pastie and ploughman's – Cheddar, pâté and Stilton – along with freshly made baps and a range of puddings. There is a traditional Sunday roast but no food is served on Sunday evening. The inn, which features in several good beer guides, includes a very pleasant enclosed garden where customers can sit and enjoy the scene. Old English roses add a splash of colour in the summer.

The Plough is open all day on Saturday and bank holidays. Children and dogs are welcome.

Telephone: 01993 868333.

How to get there: From Charlbury follow the B4022 towards Witney. Turn off at Finstock (signposted North Leigh and Wilcote) and then left (signposted North Leigh). The inn is in front of you at the next junction.

Parking: There is room to park at the rear of the pub, otherwise look for a space in the village.

Length of the walk: 4 miles. Map: OS Landranger 164 Oxford and surrounding area (GR 363162).

There are good views over the Evenlode valley on this walk. After a spell on the road the walk makes for Topples Wood and then cuts across country to the edge of Cornbury Park, part of the delightful Wychwood Forest. There is a lake to be seen here. Return to Finstock along tracks and field paths.

The Walk

Turn right, on leaving the car park, and go up the hill past a row of cottages and between hedgerows. Looking around, you will have good views of Finstock, the Evenlode valley and the rolling countryside of north-west Oxfordshire. Soon the lane curves to the right towards some cottages. When you reach a gate (Hunts Copse) turn left on to a bridleway and pass some old stables and outbuildings converted into light engineering premises.

Follow the track across the fields towards some woodland. On the right are glimpses of Wilcote House; originally a gabled Elizabethan house, Wilcote was substantially extended during the 19th century. On the Ordnance Survey map you can trace the line of Akeman Street, an old Roman road running to Bicester. Interestingly, there are two Roman villas in this part of Oxfordshire. Carry on down the track and into the trees; further down, the walk comes to a field corner. Continue with the field on the right and woodland on the left. Pheasants are likely to emerge abruptly from the undergrowth – so be warned!

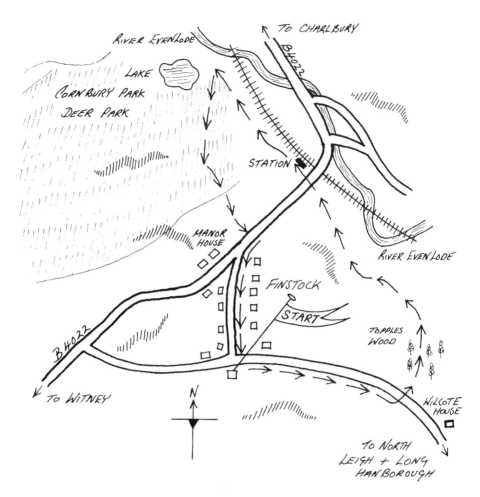

Across the fields, on the far side of the valley, lie the cottages of Stonesfield. This, unusually, is an old slate mining village; many of the stone roofing slates used in this part of Oxfordshire come from here, as do the slates of many Oxford colleges. It seems nature played an important role in the local mining industry. When a frost was expected the entire village would ensure that the stone was uncovered so that the freezing temperature would split it into slates. If the frost was at night the church bells would rouse the villagers!

Soon, the bridleway, which can be muddy, becomes enclosed by trees. When, in due course, you emerge from a tunnel of trees, with a field on the right, turn sharp right to join a path. Follow it for a few yards until you reach a field corner. Veer left into the field and follow a clear path running up the slope and parallel to the field boundary, which is between 50-100 yards over to the left. The cottages of Finstock are visible on the far side of the field.

Aim for a track and follow it with a hedgerow on the left; at the road turn left for a few yards and then right (signposted Charlbury). Follow the drive as it twists and turns and then straightens. There are good views from here over the Evenlode valley. Proceed ahead through a pleasant avenue of oak trees and on towards the edge of Cornbury Park. Pass some houses and cottages on the right and then walk on for a few yards until you reach the lake. Note the plaque set in the wall here. It reads:

> Cream of Lanfine
> Born April 10th, 1970
> Died 24th May, 1977
> Avon's best friend.

Cream of Lanfine was a dog belonging to the son of Lord Rotherwick, who lives at Cornbury Park.

If you have time to visit Charlbury or simply to stroll beside the fence of the deer park, continue along the drive for a few yards and then swing right at the gate. Retrace your steps to the lake and take the path on the right, just beyond it. Cross the paddock to the far right-hand corner. Beyond the fence join a wide grassy ride lined by trees. At the next junction of paths go straight on and after a few yards bear left at the fork. Follow the track alongside fencing. Pass some woodland and here are striking views over the Evenlode valley again. Soon the track descends to the edge of a field. Follow the edge and climb the slope towards some derelict farm buildings. As the track bends left towards them, go straight on into the grounds of a private house. The public right of way cuts diagonally right, across the lawn. Look for a gap in the hedge and go out to the road. Turn right for a few yards, then left (signposted North Leigh and Wilcote). Pass the Crown on the left and go down the lane. There are lines of cottages on the right as the road descends the hillside. Bear left (signposted North Leigh) and the Plough is facing you down at the next junction.

⑪ Woodstock
The Star

This 17th century former coaching inn opposite Woodstock Town Hall and Market Place is conveniently located for tourists visiting Blenheim Palace. The front of the building has a Georgian façade, the result of an attempt to modernise it. Inside, the inn is long and quite narrow at the front; from the outside it looks very small, but it is spacious enough to accommodate its many customers. The main bar includes a portrait of Winston Churchill. There is also a cosy log fire. The dining area is at the rear and beyond it is a courtyard. Real ale enthusiasts have a choice of Wadworth 6X, Tetley Bitter and Marston's Pedigree, while others are catered for with an extensive selection of wines, Carlsberg and Stella Artois lagers, Guinness and Dry Blackthorn cider. The lunchtime menu includes ploughman's, large baguettes, jacket potatoes with various fillings and pasta. The evening menu consists of a selection of starters – freshly made soup of the day and warm black pudding with smoked bacon salad among them; main courses include slow roasted half shoulder of lamb, chicken and vegetable pie, salmon fish cakes, tagliatelle and traditional fish and chips. There is also a choice of daily specials, a Sunday roast and a selection of desserts, including fresh fruit salad and three scoops of deluxe ice cream.

The Star is open all day throughout the year. Children are welcome, but dogs must be kept away from eating areas. Non-alcoholic beverages, including tea, coffee and hot chocolate, are also available. The inn gets very busy, especially at weekends.
Telephone: 01993 811373.

How to get there: Woodstock is on the A44 between Oxford and Stratford-upon-Avon.

Parking: There are spaces in the town. The best place, however, is the free car park off Hensington Road, which is located on the right of the A44 as you enter the town from Oxford.

Length of the walk: 5¼ miles, including the Bladon spur. Map: OS Landranger 164 Oxford and surrounding area (GR 443167).

Blenheim Palace, set in its magnificent 2000-acre parkland landscaped by Capability Brown, forms the backdrop for much of this walk. Apart from an optional spur to Bladon church, where Winston Churchill is buried, the entire route is within the boundaries of the park, providing walkers and visitors with glimpses of its many treasures.

From the market place in Woodstock it is a short walk to the Triumphal Arch, beyond which the great Baroque house, covering seven acres, can be seen across the lake. The route is along permitted drives and pathways; throughout the year there is an admission fee to the park. During the summer the charge includes various attractions. The park is open daily 9 am–4.45 pm. The gates close at 6.30 pm.

The Walk
Turn right on leaving the inn and walk along the Market Place to the Woodstock Gate – one of the main entrances to Blenheim Palace. The palace, England's largest stately home and open to the public between March and October (ring 01993 811325 for more details), took 20 years to complete. The architect John Vanbrugh was commissioned to design the house for John Churchill, 1st Duke of Marlborough, following his victory over the French at Blenheim in 1704. Inside, there are various state rooms and tapestries, the Long Library, considered by many to be the finest room in the house, and the room where Winston Churchill was born. Immediately beyond the Triumphal Arch you have a stunning view of the palace, the lake and the Grand Bridge. The immense size of the house and the vastness of its park invariably catch first-time visitors by surprise. This view is often described as the finest in England. King George III quite rightly remarked, 'We have nothing to equal this', when he first set eyes on it. It is still difficult to believe that the valley of the Glyme was no more

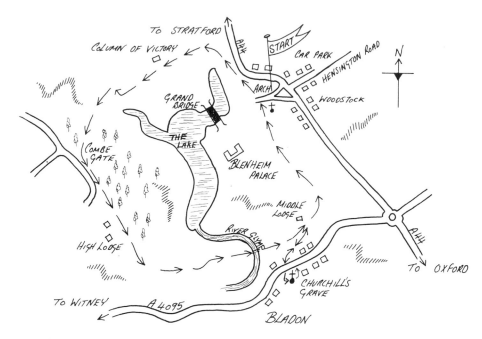

than a marshy wilderness before Capability Brown dammed the river and created the splendid lake.

Turn sharp right (pedestrians only) and follow the wide tarmac path down through the trees. From here there are spectacular views of the lake and, on the horizon, the imposing Column of Victory soaring towards the sky. The path runs alongside the boundary wall, beyond which is the main A44 Oxford – Stratford road. The graceful outline of the palace is visible on this stretch of the walk. Pass a stone-built cottage to reach a junction of paths. Swing sharp left beneath the branches of some oak trees. After a few yards veer right to join a path running up the grassy bank. Follow the path over level ground towards the Column of Victory. When you draw level with the 18th century statue of John Churchill, 1st Duke of Marlborough, there is a splendid vista of the palace glimpsed beyond an avenue of trees. Continue ahead with fencing now on your immediate right and soon you reach a drive. Cross it and join a grassy track between trees. Descend a gentle slope towards the north-west arm of the lake; at the junction, by some trees, turn right and make for a stile in the fence. Cross it and then veer right to follow the grassy path towards more trees. Soon the path curves left and joins a tarmac drive. Continue ahead on the drive and follow it through the Blenheim Estate. When you reach Combe Gate, with a lodge on the right, continue on the drive, avoiding the right-hand turning.

Proceed along the drive. On the right, between the trees, there are glimpses of the countryside around Long Hanborough and North Leigh. The route of our walk is now thickly wooded as the drive cuts between oak trees and carpets of bracken. Pass a turning on the right to High Lodge and continue along the enclosed drive. On the left are glimpses of the lake. Pass a stone-built lodge on the left. Pheasants may be seen on this stretch of the walk. Now the trees thin to provide open expanses of grass. Follow the drive to the classical stone bridge and cross the river Glyme. Keep to the drive as it now curves right. Further on, views of the palace edge into view on the left.

At the next lodge (Middle Lodge) turn sharp right and follow the drive down beside Bladon playground. Go through a kissing-gate and follow the lane into the centre of Bladon. At the main road turn right and walk along the pavement. Just before the road bends right by some cottages, take the path (there are railings here) and follow it up the left-hand bank to the lychgate at the entrance to Bladon church. Take the path along the left-hand side of the 19th century church and you will see the graves of various members of the Churchill family. Most notable among these stone and marble memorial tablets is the grave of Sir Winston Churchill (1874 – 1965). Over the years thousands of people, have visited this unremarkable country church-yard, a constant and unchanging testimony to the high regard in which this great British statesman and wartime leader is held.

Walk on through the churchyard and exit at the gate. Note the plaque in the wall: 'Presented by Oxfordshire Blacksmiths in token of their respect for Sir Winston Churchill, 1965.'

Turn left, and go down the lane, beside the primary school. At the main road bear left and then immediately right into Park Lane and retrace your steps through the Blenheim Palace Estate to Middle Lodge. Swing right at this point, go through a gate beside a cattle grid and at the next junction turn left. There are wide views over the parkland, dotted with trees; in the distance, slightly to your right, you can see the church tower at Woodstock. On the left along this stretch is the entrance to the pleasure gardens, herb garden and cafeteria. During the summer you have the option of travelling on the narrow-gauge railway, which runs parallel to the drive at this point.

Go through a white gate and, with the palace now clearly visible over to the left, continue ahead following the pedestrian way-out sign. Head for the Triumphal Arch and return to Woodstock, passing the entrance to Oxfordshire County Museum just before the Star. The museum includes a fascinating and comprehensive record of Oxfordshire's crafts and industries down the years.

12 Thrupp
The Boat Inn

Thrupp is little more than a row of pretty cottages on the Oxford Canal, one of the earliest of our inland waterways. It took 20 years to complete and was finished in 1790. Beginning near Coventry, it never extended south of Oxford, where it joins the Thames. Today, it is especially popular with boating enthusiasts. Thrupp and a stretch of the waterway featured prominently in one of the televised *Inspector Morse* mysteries, *The Riddle of the Third Mile*, in which a body surfaced in the canal!

The Boat Inn, picturesquely situated beside the canal, is understood to be about 300 years old. It certainly predates the canal era, though because of its position it is chiefly associated with the waterway and has served generations of boatmen and bargees down the years. The roof structure includes some very old timbers and the smaller bar, known as the Captain's Cabin, was once the local shop. In recent years the inn also featured in the above mentioned episode of *Inspector Morse*. As well as the Captain's Cabin, there is the Bosun's Bar, which includes various watercolours of the nearby lift bridge and one or two rural scenes. There is also a very good oil painting of the inn.

Real ales include Morrells Varsity and Bitter, and there are Harp and Harp Extra lagers, Guinness and Stowford Press draught cider. The menu is good and quite imaginative: sandwiches and ploughman's; Thrupp crusties, which consist of French bread filled with ham, beef, chicken, salad or cheese; starters, including soup of the day, egg mayonnaise and prawn cocktail; plus omelettes, vegetarian dishes, grills, various salads and fish dishes. The evening menu is more extensive. On Sunday the traditional roast is supplemented by a limited alternative menu, which includes the ploughman's and sandwiches.

There is a large, enclosed garden at the rear. Children are welcome in the Bosun's Bar, but no dogs please. The inn gets very busy on summer weekends and bank holidays. Larger groups should book for Sunday lunch.

Telephone: 01865 374279.

How to get there: Take the A34 to Kidlington, then the A4260 towards Banbury. The turning to Thrupp is on the right.

Parking: There is room to park at the inn and also space nearby.

Length of the walk: 3½ miles. Map: OS Landranger 164 Oxford and surrounding area (GR 481158).

Beyond Hampton Poyle the walk reaches the old abandoned village of Hampton Gay. Here you will see the remains of an old manor house, which was ravaged by fire in 1887. The final stretch of the walk is along a towpath between the Oxford Canal and the river Cherwell to Thrupp Wide. There are usually plenty of narrow boats to see here.

The Walk

From the front door of the Boat Inn turn left and walk along the lane. On the left is a row of picturesque cottages overlooking the Oxford Canal. The cottages were built to accommodate canal workers. Proceed as far as the lift bridge and cross it to enter the boat maintenance yard, following the sign for Oxfordshire County Council's 'Kidlington circular walk'. Pass to the right of some thatched cottages and disregard a stile on the right. Walk ahead and pass under the railway bridge to reach a gate. Go straight on along a clear path which cuts through woodland plantations established with recreation, wildlife and conservation in mind and supported by the Forestry Authority of England and the Forestry Commission. Keep to the path running between the plantations; the river Cherwell is close by on the left. Disregard several stiles on the right,

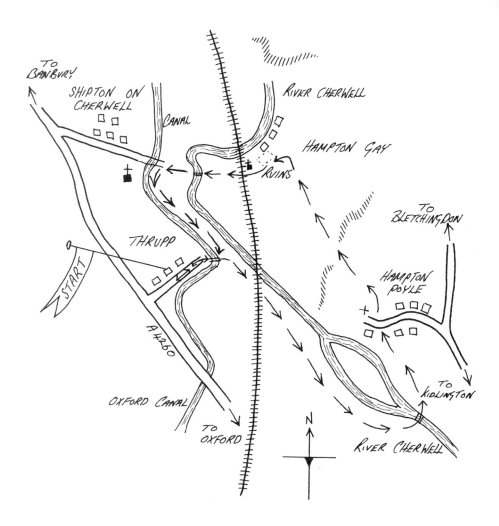

pass through a wrought iron gate and, beyond the new woodlands, follow a field boundary path alongside lines of ancient willow trees by the river. The soaring 15th-century spire of Kidlington church can be seen across the fields to the right. Draw level with the spire and then continue for a short distance until you reach a footbridge spanning the Cherwell. Head for the opposite bank, cross the double stile and footbridge and make for the stile in the next boundary, aiming for the left-hand corner of the garden of a bow-fronted house. Head diagonally across this field and emerge at the road at Hampton Poyle, an isolated village overlooking the floodplain. Hampton is derived from an old English word for 'homestead'. Nearby is the village church and a brief detour – only a matter of yards – brings you to the churchyard. Stepping just inside the gate you will see a seat in memory of Mary Ann Bickley and Ernest Charles Bickley. Their graves are opposite the seat.

Return to the road and then bear left (signposted Kidlington circular walk). Cross a field of coarse grass and rough pasture. Go over another double stile with a ditch in between and enter the next field. Follow the left-hand boundary for a few yards until you reach two more stiles. Cross over them, disregard the path running on the extreme right and take the waymarked path (CW) diagonally right. Two gates are visible in the boundary. Make for the left-hand gate, turn immediately left across a paddock to another stile. Follow the next arrow, aiming half-right to the top corner of the field. Go over another stile, over a ditch and through the hedgerow into the next field.

Follow a clear path diagonally right across the field towards a line of trees. Pass over two wooden footbridges and head out across the field towards the gap in the far boundary hedge. In the next field aim slightly left, still following the CW symbols. In the next boundary cross another stile and walk towards the buildings of Hampton Gay, keeping the fence on your left. Ahead of you, amid the trees on the far side of the field, are the ruins of the manor at Hampton Gay.

As you approach the ruined house, swing left on to a grassy path and follow it down under some power lines. On the right, near the railway line, is St Giles church. The key to the church is available from Manor Farm or Manor Cottage. The history of the church is described in some detail outside, as are the circumstances of a terrible rail disaster on the nearby line in 1874. A train was travelling to the Midlands on Christmas Eve when the carriages left the track and plunged down the embankment. Thirty passengers were killed and Queen Victoria sent a message of sympathy. Lord Randolph Churchill arrived from Blenheim Palace to help, three weeks after the birth of his son, Winston.

From the church make for the stile and white fence, and cross the railway line. Head towards some trees on the far side of the field, with the church tower at Shipton-on-Cherwell now visible. Look for a footbridge over the river, cross it and then walk ahead across a field. On the far side you join a track. Follow it for a few yards until you begin to approach a bridge over the canal. At this point veer left, down the bank and on to the towpath. Walk ahead along a stretch where there are often lines of brightly painted narrow boats moored. Soon, looking back, you will have an impressive view of the church, once known as the bargees' church, standing proudly on the opposite bank. Continue on the towpath, following it as it slices between the canal on the right and the Cherwell on the left. The towpath curves to the right at Thrupp Wide; cross the lift bridge again and retrace your steps to the Boat Inn.

13 Beckley
The Abingdon Arms

The village of Beckley is delightful. Near the 14th century church rows of crooked stone houses and thatched cottages cling to the hillside, 400 ft above Otmoor.

Some fascinating artefacts can be seen at the popular Abingdon Arms, situated high above Otmoor, among them a pictorial map of the city of Oxford and an old relief map of Oxfordshire. Additionally there is an aerial view of Otmoor and Beckley, as well as some splendid black and white photographs of the village, the church and the inn: a permanent reminder of how English village life in bygone days used to be. Not a great deal is known about the history of the pub, though it is thought to date back to the mid-17th century. Evelyn Waugh spent his honeymoon here in 1928, having probably discovered the inn while he was a student at Oxford and may have stayed here whilst writing *Decline and Fall*.

Real ales on handpump include Adnams Bitter and a guest beer. Tetley, John Bull keg, Guinness and Copper Head draught cider are also on offer. The superior menu will certainly appeal to those who appreciate good food. In winter the choice includes smoked salmon pâté, avocado prawns and chilli mayonnaise, or you may find Thai

chicken curry; sliced smoked chicken; tagliolini with sun-dried tomatoes, pine-nuts and wild mushroom sauce with Parmesan cheese. The evening menu varies slightly. The summer menu, which is essentially cold, includes fresh crab, Greek salad, farmhouse duck liver terrine and home-cooked ham. There is no food on Sunday evening throughout the year. Children over 14 are welcome; dogs on leads please. There is an extensive sloping garden with a floodlit terrace, groves of fruit trees, a summer house and various willows and shrubs.
Telephone: 01865 351311.

How to get there: Beckley is just off the B4027, between Islip and Wheatley. The Abingdon Arms is in the centre of the village, just to the east of the church.

Parking: The inn has a car park, or you can park in Beckley – space permitting.

Length of the walk: 2¾ miles. Map: OS Landranger 164 Oxford and surrounding area (GR 565113).

From the village the walk follows the Oxfordshire Way down to Noke Wood. There are glorious views from here over Otmoor – a curious, primitive landscape imbued with a strange, ghostly stillness. It is claimed the Reverend Charles Dodgson, otherwise known as Lewis Carroll, was inspired by the view of this low-lying, empty wilderness of 4,000 acres to write about the giant chessboard in Alice through the Looking Glass.
During the Second World War bombing practice took place on Otmoor and even today there is a rifle range here. The RSPB is restoring part of Otmoor's wetland to encourage many different bird species to use it as a habitat. The walk runs along the southern edge of Otmoor before returning to Beckley.

The Walk
From the Abingdon Arms turn right and walk along the High Street between lines of cottages and bungalows. On the left is an old red pre-British Telecom telephone box. Soon the road bends sharp left. As it does so, turn right by the church into Church Street. Note the lychgate here. Follow the lane down between rows of stone cottages, some of which are thatched. Pass the entrance to Beckley Church of England primary school; further down there are glimpses of Otmoor between the trees and hedgerows. Continue down the green lane towards the vast green expanse and soon you reach a stile on the left. Take the path into the field. This stretch of the walk coincides briefly with the Oxfordshire Way. Cross into the next field via a stile and then head diagonally right. There are magnificent views of Otmoor from here.

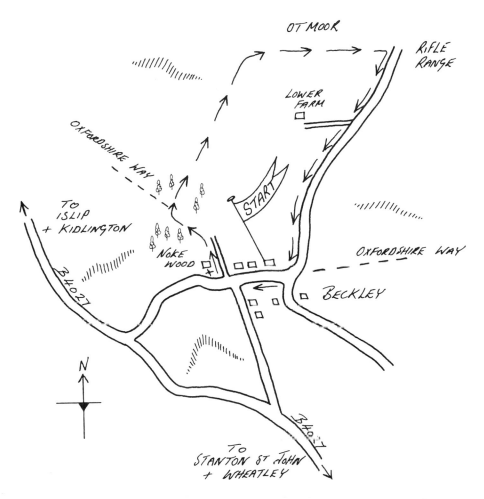

Walk down the field and look for a stile in the bottom right corner.
Join a muddy path and follow it to the right. Soon it bends left into
Noke Wood.

After a few yards you emerge from the trees on the edge of a field.
Turn right and follow the grassy boundary, leaving the route of the
Oxfordshire Way, which now heads west. Follow the wide path for
some distance; the trees of Noke Wood are on the right. Eventually,
at the corner of the wood, the path curves to the right. Follow it round
to the right, pass a field gateway and continue with hedge and ditch
on the right. After about 150 yards cross a footbridge on the right and

continue to another footbridge in the left-hand corner of the field. There are good views here of Beckley up on the hillside.

Turn left, then right after about 100 yards. Follow the right-hand edge of a ploughed field; this bridleway can be rather wet and muddy at times. Pass a gateway on the right and continue. On a cold winter's day and even sometimes in high summer, you can sense the ghostly atmosphere of Otmoor. It is a bleak place in any season, at times reminiscent of East Anglia with its flat, empty fields, ditches and dykes.

In the field corner join a track. Just before it reaches some double gates veer right, through some trees and over a footbridge to reach a hard path. Turn right and follow the path between hedgerows. Soon you reach a single-track lane running to Beckley. Follow the lane and in a while you pass the turning to Lower Farm. Continue ahead towards Beckley and soon the lane climbs between various houses and cottages on the edge of the village. Beckley church tower can be seen over to the right amid the trees. Follow the lane round to the right by some cottages and now you briefly rejoin the route of the Oxfordshire Way. Follow the lane for a short distance and the Abingdon Arms is on the right at the junction.

14 Oxford
The Eagle and Child

In order to see everything that Oxford has to offer, you would probably have to go back again and again – and even then there is always something new to stumble upon. As well as the colleges, there are many other historic buildings and monuments to see. Apart from the city's priceless treasures, there are, of course, always the tourists. Autumn and winter are probably quieter but whenever you visit Oxford, 'that sweet city with her dreaming spires' is sure to be a memorable experience.

The first thing that strikes you about the fascinating Eagle and Child inn is that it is extremely long and narrow in shape. The pub dates back to around 1650, when it was named after the crest of the Earl of Derby, who owned land in Oxford. A carved motif depicts the Derby coronet, beneath which is an eagle holding in its claws a basket in which there is a baby. Over the years the inn has become affectionately known as the 'Bird and Baby' or the 'Bird and Brat', particularly by students!

During the Civil War the pub became a payhouse for the Royalist Army. Several centuries later, between 1939 and 1962, J.R.R. Tolkien and C.S. Lewis met every Tuesday morning in the back room – known as the Rabbit Room – to drink and to discuss their work. Many old photographs of C.S. Lewis, Charles Williams and other dons from that period adorn the walls. More recently the inn has appeared in a television episode of *Inspector Morse*, disguised as a wine bar.

The real ales at this pub include Burton Ale, Marston's Pedigree, Tetley Bitter and a running guest ale. Lagers include Lowenbrau and Carlsberg and there is also Dry Blackthorn cider. The bar menu is straightforward but appetising. Platters are piled with salad, pickles and fresh crusty bread, and a range of jacket potatoes and vegetarian dishes is available. Traditional meals include scampi, Cumberland sausage and Cajun chicken; one of the inn's most popular dishes is a giant Yorkshire pudding with chilli and sausage. A traditional Sunday roast is also available and there is a specials board. The Eagle and Child, which includes a no smoking area, attracts a good mix of locals, students and tourists and is typical of Oxford's many historic and distinctive inns. The pub is open all day, though food is not available in the evening. No dogs when meals are being served.

Telephone: 01865 310154.

How to get there: Oxford is well served by trains and a network of major routes, including the M40, A40 and A34. The inn is in St Giles.

Parking: The Eagle and Child does not have a car park. However, it might be possible to find a space nearby at certain times of the day.

If you are intending to spend most of the day in Oxford, then try the 'park and ride'.

Length of the walk: 2 ¼ miles. Map: OS Landranger 164 Oxford and surrounding area (GR 511067).

The city walk I have chosen begins in St Giles, then heads for Christ Church Meadow and the river Cherwell. Soon you reach the Botanic Garden and on a sunny summer's day you are likely to see punters unsteadily manoeuvring their craft through adjacent Magdalen Bridge. The walk now heads for New College, the Bodleian Library and the Radcliffe Camera before returning to St Giles.

The Walk

Leaving the inn bear right and walk along St Giles, Oxford's widest street and used for ceremonies and processions. Charles I drilled his men here during the Civil War. If time permits, you might like to visit St John's College on the opposite side of the street. The college, which was founded in 1437 for Cistercian monks, is open every day between 1 pm and 5 pm and includes a glorious garden beyond the Front Quad and the Canterbury Quad.

From the entrance to St John's College walk down to the Martyrs' Memorial, commemorating the 16th century Protestant martyrs who were burned at the stake in nearby Broad Street. Opposite here is the Randolph Hotel. Follow Magdalen Street and over the crossroads into Cornmarket Street, which is pedestrianised, so you can wander freely among the shops and buildings. However, look out for buses!

On the left is the church of St Michael at the North Gate; its Saxon tower is the oldest building in Oxford and originally linked the city wall and the North Gate. From the top there is a magnificent close-up view of Oxford.

Soon you reach Carfax, the junction with St Aldates and the High Street ('The High'). This is the very heart of Oxford, where four streets converge – Carfax is the Latin 'quadrifurcus' meaning 'four-forked'. Carfax Tower is where Charles II was proclaimed King in May 1660. Walk ahead into St Aldates and pass Oxford City Council's Town Hall offices; beyond this building is the Museum of Oxford – a journey through Oxford's past. On the opposite side of the street is the Civic Tourist Information Office. A visit here is well worthwhile in order to arm yourself with maps, leaflets and other general information to complete a city tour and make it that much more enjoyable.

Further along St Aldates is the entrance to Christ Church, the largest college in Oxford and founded in 1525 by Cardinal Wolsey. When he was disgraced it was refounded as King Henry VIII College. Later it became known as Christ Church when the college and the cathedral

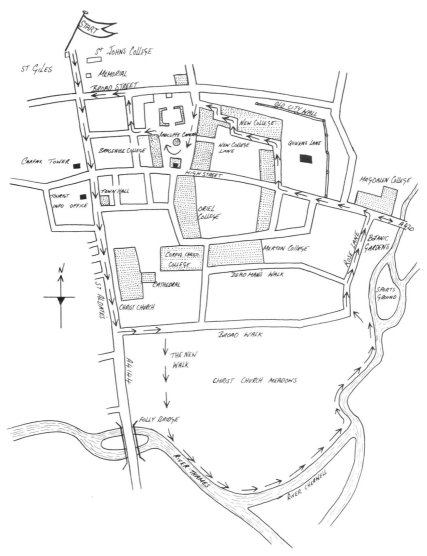

became one. Over the years Christ Church has had many notable students, including three Prime Ministers: Robert Peel, William Gladstone and Lord Salisbury. John Wesley, Lewis Carroll and W.H. Auden also studied here. The cathedral's proper title is The Cathedral Church of Christ in Oxford and not only is it the smallest of all English cathedrals but it is also the college chapel of Christ Church – making it unique in the history of the city. The steeple is believed to be the first ever built in this country. The public are welcome to visit the cathedral, chapter house and hall. Entry is through the adjacent memorial garden, opposite the Newman Mowbray bookshop.

Leave Christ Church by the Meadows exit and walk straight ahead down the tree-lined New Walk. On the left is the great green expanse of Christ Church Meadow. It is held in trust by Christ Church and was originally given by Lady Montacute to maintain her Chantry in the Lady Chapel at the Priory of St Frideswide (Christ Church Cathedral).

Soon you reach the Thames towpath, where you swing left and follow the river bank. After several minutes veer left where the river Cherwell flows into the Thames. There is a steeply arched footbridge here. On the left are striking views of the Oxford skyline beyond Christ Church Meadow. Follow the tree-lined towpath.

The river meanders between the meadows and sports fields – a peaceful backwater where you can stroll unhurried and yet remain within the shadow of the city. Pass the Broad Walk on the left and continue ahead. Oxford's magnificent backdrop of 'dreaming spires' is clearly seen and admired from here. Leave the river bank and pass through some wrought-iron gates into Rose Lane. At the junction with the High turn right towards Magdalen Bridge. On the right here is the entrance to the University Botanic Garden. The garden was founded in 1621 by the Earl of Danby. It was established on the site of a 13th century Jewish burial ground. It is the oldest botanic garden in Britain and in over 300 years plants have been grown here for both teaching and research at the University. The 8,000 different species here demonstrate the enormous diversity within the plant kingdom.

On leaving the garden you can stroll along to the Magdalen College bell tower, one of Oxford's great landmarks. During the Civil War Royalist forces defended the bridge by throwing rocks from the top of the tower down on to the heads of Parliamentarians below. Return to the Botanic Garden and continue along The High. Cross the road, pass Longwall Street and then bear right into Queen's Lane. The high perimeter wall of Queen's College is on the left and on the right are St Edmund Hall and the former parish church of St Peter-in-the-East.

Continue into New College Lane and on the right, beyond the arch, is the entrance to New College. Founded in 1379 by William of Wykeham, the college includes one of the oldest quadrangles in Oxford. The gatehouse was where the Warden used to monitor the comings and goings of his students. New College is open to the public; the gardens are bordered on two sides by the ancient city wall. Continue along New College Lane. An interesting account of Oxford's history can be found further on near the famous and outstanding Bridge of Sighs. This 1914 structure, a replica of its Venice namesake, connects the north and south quadrangles of Hertford College.

In front of you, at the junction, is the Sheldonian Theatre. The building was designed by Christopher Wren – his first major work – and was opened in 1669. Named after Gilbert Sheldon, the 17th century Archbishop of Canterbury, the theatre was built to hold important university meetings and ceremonies. Close to the Sheldonian Theatre are the buildings of the Bodleian Library. Founded by Sir Thomas Bodley, a retired civil servant, it is the second-largest library in Britain and contains five million volumes. Turn left and then bear right immediately beyond the Radcliffe Camera in Radcliffe Square. The name of Dr John Radcliffe, physician to Queen Anne, is immortalised all over Oxford. In this instance, Radcliffe left a sum of money for the building of the first round library in the country. Cross the cobbles of the square to 16th century Brasenose College, which probably took its name from a brazen door-knocker in the shape of a nose, and then bear left into Brasenose Lane. Walk along to Turl Street, then veer right and head for Broad Street where you can visit the world famous Blackwell's Bookshop. Head west along Broad Street and soon you will reach St Giles' where the walk began.

15 Horspath
The Queen's Head

Horspath is claimed to be the first true village east of Oxford. It boasts some picturesque cottages and period houses. The stone building of the Queen's Head is about 300 years old and includes various black and white photographs of the village. The lounge bar has been extended to provide a dining area with non-smoking tables, and the games room includes bar billiards. There are facilities for the disabled and the garden has recently been landscaped to include seating and a new paved area. There is also a children's play area, as well as a pets' corner – home to a pot bellied pig!

Real ales at the Queen's Head include Tetley Bitter, Morrells Varsity and a guest beer. There are also Lowenbrau, Castlemaine XXXX and Carlsberg lagers, as well as Strongbow and Scrumpy Jack draught cider. Food is available every day and includes various light meals, 'snack attacks', ploughman's, soup and hot baguettes. For something more substantial you could choose ham, egg and chips, fish and chips, honey roast leg of pork, steak or hot chicken salad from an extensive menu. For Sunday there is a traditional roast. Well-behaved dogs are welcome. A small brewery, based at the inn, is proposed for 1998.

Telephone: 01865 875567.

How to get there: Horspath is about 1 mile to the east of the Oxford ring road. Follow the A4192 to Cowley and then take the Horspath road at the roundabout. Turn left at the village green and then immediately right into Church Road.

Parking: There is room to park at the inn, and some spaces elsewhere in the village.

Length of the walk: 3¼ miles. Map: OS Landranger 164 Oxford and surrounding area (GR 573048).

From the village the walk makes for Shotover Plain which was once the haunt of highwaymen. An Oxford don was once attacked by a wild boar in this area. He apparently defended himself with a volume of Aristotle, using it to fend off the beast and yelling 'Graeca cum est' which roughly translated means 'with the compliments of the Greeks'. Shotover Country Park, through which the walk passes, is a popular recreational area. The soil is sandy and the hills are wooded and bracken-covered. Various trails and waymarked paths cut through the bluebells and between cherry trees and blackberries.

The Walk

From the front of the inn turn right and go up the lane. Pass Fords Close and Wrightson Close, then Butts Road. Continue into Blenheim Road, following the lane as it twists and turns between various houses, cottages and bungalows. Eventually the road ends, at the point where you join a broad bridleway running up towards some woodland. There are paddocks on the left and right of the track.

Pass one of the entrances to Shotover Country Park and continue on the bridleway. The track climbs quite steeply now, running alongside the trees of the country park. On the higher ground the route of our walk cuts through a pleasant rural landscape of fields, trees and hedgerows. When you reach a junction bear left and on your immediate left is the embankment of a reservoir. The track cuts between hedgerows and is quite wide at this point. On the right are good views over undulating countryside stretching towards Stanton St John and the bleak vastness of Otmoor beyond.

Further on, as you reach Shotover Plain, the track cuts between wide grassy verges lined by trees. Against this peaceful, unspoilt landscape of trees, fields and grassy expanses, it is hard to believe that

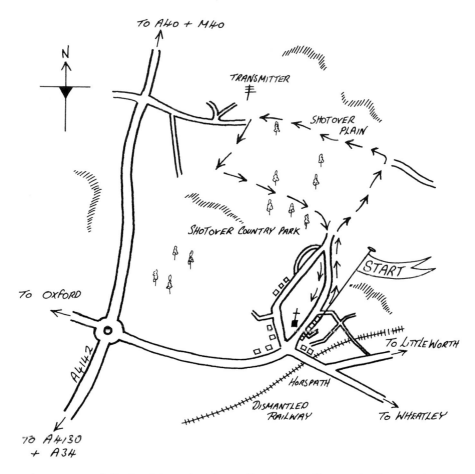

To A40 + M40

N

TRANSMITTER

SHOTOVER PLAIN

SHOTOVER COUNTRY PARK

START

To OXFORD

A4142

To LITTLEWORTH

HORSPATH

DISMANTLED RAILWAY

To WHEATLEY

To A4130 + A34

the centre of Oxford is only about 3 miles to the west. Keep going along the track, strewn with potholes, and make for the transmitter up ahead. Pass a footpath to Sandhills on the right and continue beyond the car parking area and public conveniences.

Follow the hard road between the trees and after a few yards, just before you reach the transmitter, turn left at a wooden gate (a sign here requests cyclists to keep to the bridle-path). Go down the grassy slopes; ahead of you in the distance lie the suburbs of Oxford. The car plant at Cowley is visible as you descend the hill.

There are picnic tables and benches in this part of the country park, making this is an ideal venue for a short break from the walk. Further down the slopes you reach a junction of paths; veer right to join a wide grassy path and follow it down between gorse bushes. At the bottom of the slope you reach a junction with a woodland path. Turn left and walk along the path; it drops down steeply and then rises again just as sharply. Either side of the path are trees and carpets of bracken. At a junction of paths continue ahead. The main path runs like an artery through a network of secondary routes; branch paths and turnings shoot off into the undergrowth at regular intervals. Note the sandy soil underfoot. Peering ahead you can see the route of the walk climbing the slopes of the far hillside.

The path drops down steeply between bracken clumps and thickets of gorse bushes. Climb the next slope and at the top cross over a track and continue. Descend and then rise once more and at this point it is worth pausing to look back over a wide area of the country park. When you reach another path cutting across our route, with a waymarker post on the left, turn right. Follow the path through some oak and silver birch trees and veer left at the fork. Pass over a track, disregard a turning on the left and then drop down steeply towards lines of trees. On reaching the trees, bear right and then curve left towards a footbridge. A paddock is visible up on the hillside. Follow the path along the woodland edge. The trees here mark the boundary of the park. On the right is a concrete track. Go on down to another footbridge in the corner of the wood, then out to the bridleway followed near the start of this walk. Turn right and return to the village of Horspath, reaching the inn on the left.

16 Kelmscott
The Plough

The village, overlooking the peaceful watermeadows of the upper Thames, is famous as the summer home of William Morris, the 19th century writer, craftsman and artist. Morris, a renowned idealist, wanted to achieve social harmony and create a sort of rural Utopia where men and women lived and worked together in perfect unison and there was no such thing as mass production. Morris died in 1896 and is buried in Kelmscott churchyard.

Built in 1690, the Plough reopened in 1993 after a period of closure. The inn has been extensively modernised and improved and now includes eight en suite bedrooms. Thankfully, many of the pub's original features, including the stone floor and the oak beams, have been preserved. There are three bars – one of which used to house the village shop and post office. The bar menu is varied and appetising with dishes such as tomato, wine and mint soup, fresh fish, pâté and toast, plus sandwiches and ploughman's, salads, jacket potatoes, basket meals and children's dishes, plaice and chips, scampi and chips, buckwheat pancakes and home-cooked ham, egg and chips. Home-made desserts include banana split, cheesecake, peach melba and apple flapjack. The specials board usually includes beef and steak pie,

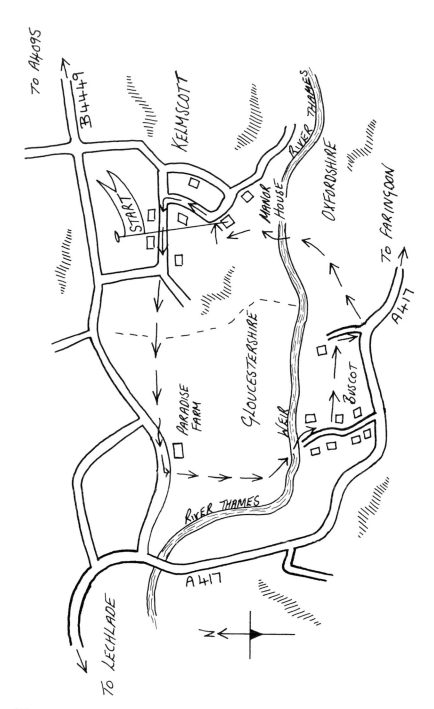

TO A409S

B4449

KELMSCOTT

RIVER THAMES

START

MANOR HOUSE

OXFORDSHIRE

TO FARINGDON

A417

GLOUCESTERSHIRE

BUSCOT

PARADISE FARM

WEIR

RIVER THAMES

A417

TO LECHLADE

N

fresh haddock, and kidneys in Madeira sauce. Steak, trout and gammon are also available. On Sunday there is a traditional roast.

Real ales including Morland Original and a guest ale, with Dry Blackthorn cider, and Foster's and Stella Artois lagers also provided. Children are welcome, but dogs are allowed only in the public bar. Outside is a beer garden and patio with tables and chairs. The inn is open all day in summer. Though Kelmscott is somewhat off the beaten track, it does attract many visitors and tourists in summer, so expect the Plough to be busy, particularly at weekends.

Telephone: 01367 253543.

How to get there: Follow the A417 between Faringdon and Lechlade and turn right at the Gloucestershire county sign (signposted Kelmscott). Follow the signs for the village and the inn. The Plough is on the right.

Parking: There is room to park at the inn or nearby in the village.

Length of the walk: 4¼ miles. Map: OS Landranger 163 Cheltenham and Cirencester (GR 248991).

The walk cuts across country to cross the Thames at Buscot weir and lock, a picturesque spot, and then heads back to Kelmscott. The path recrosses the river just before reaching the village. Part of the walk is in neighbouring Gloucestershire.

The Walk
To visit Kelmscott Manor turn right on leaving the inn and then bear left. Follow the lane between stone houses and cottages, pass Coles Barn and at the junction turn right. The manor is on the right. It is open to the public every Wednesday and on the third Saturday of each month between 1st April and 30th September; group bookings may be made on some other days. For full details write to the Administrator, or telephone 01367 252486.

Return to the inn and continue along the road, heading in a northerly direction out of the village. At the junction swing left by the church and follow the quiet lane. Pass Church Cottage and Home Lea. When the lane bends right go straight on into the field on the right of the track. Cross the field diagonally and at the footbridge cross into the next field. The stream here links the river Leach and the Thames and forms the county boundary between Oxfordshire and Gloucestershire. Go straight on towards the corner of the field where there is a hedge on the right.

Cross the stile into the next field and walk along the field edge. The hedge is on your immediate right. Pass through the gate in the corner and continue across the next field towards the stile in the far boundary, with a farm over to the left. At the stile go out to the road and bear left. Pass the farm buildings and continue beyond several bungalows.

Pass a cottage called Greenacres and bear left to join a muddy waymarked track running alongside farm buildings. Follow the well signposted track across the fields towards a line of trees. In the distance are gently swelling hills and woods. At a stream by the line of trees bend right for a few yards and then go left and over several footbridges. Cross the meadows by veering half-left towards the Thames footbridge at Buscot Lock. Over to the right the great soaring spire of Lechlade church stands out on the horizon. Cross the footbridge and then go straight ahead to the next footbridge by Buscot Weir. Turn left at the sign 'Buscot Water Treatment Works'. Walk along the narrow lane beside some riverside seats and after a few yards, at a ditch, swing left and walk along the edge of the meadows. Cross a footbridge and then walk ahead along the right-hand boundary of the field. Pass an opening into a field on the right and continue.

In the field corner aim a little to the right and then walk along the left-hand edge of the adjacent field, keeping several stone cottages and some trees on the left. In the corner go through the gate and then turn right. Follow the green lane between hedgerows and fields. On reaching a bend of the main A417 road swing left immediately to join a waymarked path. Follow it to the far corner of the field, either diagonally or by completing two sides of it. Look for the waymarker disc at the gateway into the next field and cut across to some trees. The next disc is visible amid them.

Cross a footbridge and then veer half-right into the adjoining field. Follow the left edge of the field, keeping the hedgerow on your immediate left. The Thames can now be seen pottering through a pleasing landscape of meadows, fields and woodland. Make for the far corner of the field where a footbridge takes you into the field on the left. Aim half-right now and walk towards a white building and a footbridge over the river. At the next boundary join a track and follow it to the river, crossing a stile and then the footbridge. Narrow boats and cruisers can be seen lining the river bank here.

On the far bank of the river turn right to the stile and then leave the river bank by following the field edge, keeping the fence on your left. Go over several footbridges; at the field edge swing left for several yards into the adjoining field and then right to follow its right-hand boundary. The houses of Kelmscott are visible now. In the field corner turn right and walk along a grassy path between hedgerows and ditches. Pass various entrances to houses and cottages and soon you reach the inn where the walk began.

72

Tadpole Bridge, Buckland Marsh
The Trout Inn

The Trout is a family-owned freehouse and has been a pub for over 100 years. Its delightful Thames-side setting makes it a very popular place in summer. The garden is extensive and the Trout also offers two miles of fishing rights downstream and several camp sites. At one time there was a wharf at the bottom of the garden and the inn itself used to accommodate bargees transporting coal.

Inside, there is a bar and separate dining areas with flagstones, stone walls and photographs of river scenes. Real ales include Morlands Tanners Jack, Fuller's London Pride and Archers Village Bitter, while cider lovers can opt for Scrumpy Jack. Guinness, Carlsberg, Kronenbourg and Stella Artois are also available. Food is served every day and everything is home cooked to order, ranging from light snacks to a full à la carte menu. There is soup, sandwiches with various fillings, baguettes in summer, toasted sandwiches, baked potatoes and ploughman's. More substantial dishes include 8 oz Aberdeen Angus rump steak, smoked chicken, scampi and chips, ham, egg and chips, curry, chilli con carne and steak and kidney pie. There is also a good range of puddings and a Sunday roast. Well-behaved dogs and children are welcome but no dogs in the eating area. Booking is

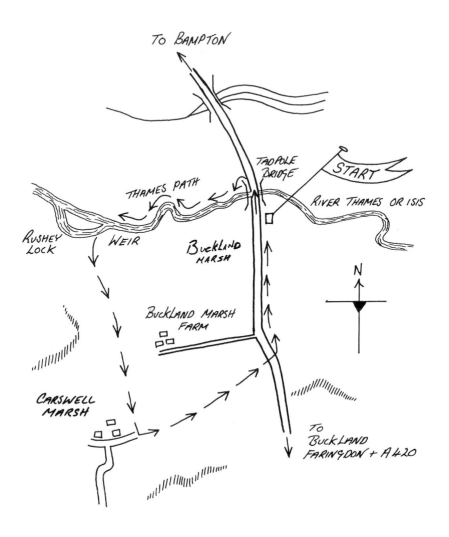

preferred for the evening. The Trout is closed on Sunday evening between 1st January and Easter.

Telephone: 01367 870382.

How to get there: From Faringdon follow the A420 towards Oxford and Abingdon. Turn left (signposted Buckland and Bampton) and the inn will be found on the right after about 2 miles.

Parking: The best place to park is at the inn's car park. The road at the front of the Trout is not really suitable for parking.

Length of the walk: 3¼ miles. Map: OS Landranger 164 Oxford and surrounding area (GR 335004).

The delightfully named Tadpole Bridge marks the start of this fairly short walk in the upper Thames valley. It is easy going all the way, with no hills to climb. The isolated surroundings can be a bit bleak; a sunny afternoon or summer evening are probably the best times to try it. Near the start is Rushey Lock, where there is a spectacular weir. For the first mile the walk follows the route of the Thames path.

The Walk

From the inn go out to the road and turn right. Go over Tadpole Bridge and then bear left to join the waymarked footpath. Fishermen are often glimpsed along this quiet stretch of the upper Thames or Isis. The surroundings are peaceful, rural and essentially undisturbed. The river twists and turns beside you. Pass a concrete pillbox and continue on the Thames path. On reaching the buildings at Rushey Lock, turn left through the gate (dogs on leads please). Cross the river by means of the footbridge at the lock gates, turn right for a few yards then left over another footbridge above the weir. (This is a permitted path by kind permission of the National Rivers Authority.) The river plunges over the weir in spectacular fashion and the sound of it is so intense that it is likely to make conversation very difficult.

Once over the bridge cross a stile and then veer half-right towards a gap in the hedgerow. Pass through it and then bear right and follow the field boundary. Cross a footbridge and then a stile into the next field. Continue along the field edge, pass under some pylons and then cross into the next field. The buildings of Buckland Marsh Farm can be seen over to the left.

Up ahead now are the buildings of Carswell, a hamlet of isolated cottages; in the distance is a low ridge of hills beyond which is the Vale of the White Horse. In the field corner go into the next field and then immediately turn left beside the cottages of Carswell to join a bridleway. Follow the path along the field edge. Gently rising wooded slopes are to your right. On the left are rows of beech trees.

Cross over a track and then walk ahead along the left-hand edge of the field in front of you. At the next field go straight on to the far boundary. Make for a gate at right angles to the fence; go through it and then turn right to follow the right-hand edge of the field. The road and various buildings are visible up ahead.

In the field corner go through a gate and out to the road. Turn left and walk along this sometimes busy road for about ¾ mile. Pass the entrance to Buckland Marsh Farm, then a waymarked footpath on the right and continue along the road to the inn.

18 Longworth
The Blue Boar

John Fell, Dean of Christ Church and Bishop of Oxford, was born in Longworth in the early 17th century. One of his students based a famous Latin epigram on him following a reprimand:

> I do not love thee Doctor Fell,
> The reason why I cannot tell.
> But this I know and know full well
> I do not love thee Doctor Fell.

The novelist R.D. Blackmore, best known for *Lorna Doone*, was born in the village in 1825.

The delightful partly thatched Blue Boar inn was originally a bakery and an Elizabethan alehouse. In more recent times it featured in the television series *Private Shultz* starring Michael Elphick. The quaint main bar has much to divert the attention, including a collection of antique wooden skis dating back to the 1920s, a splendid 1981 painting of the inn and a strong pugilistic theme with many old boxing prints. There are cosy fires, high-backed settles, pews, beams and stone walls, as well as various brass artefacts. There is a small ante-room with prints and photographs of horse racing scenes.

The Blue Boar is a Morrells pub and the real ales on handpump include Morrells Bitter and Varsity. There is also Guinness, Stowford Press cider and Kronenbourg lager. Food is available seven days a week and starters includes home-made soup, garlic mushrooms, deep fried squid, smoked salmon and scrambled eggs. Main dishes range from Thai chicken curry, grilled calves' liver with smoked bacon, 8 oz fillet steak, 12 oz rump steak and battered cod. Camembert and the choice of steaks are the inn's speciality dishes. Sticky toffee pudding is also a big favourite and according to a previous landlord the Blue Boar was the first pub ever to serve it. Booking is advised at weekends, well behaved children and dogs are welcome and there is a beer garden as well as tables and benches at the front.

Telephone: 01865 820494.

How to get there: Follow the A420 between Oxford and Faringdon. Look out for the signs for Longworth and follow them into Longworth village. The inn is in the centre of the village, in Tucks Lane.

Parking: There is a small car park at the inn, and some spaces where you can park in the village.

Length of the walk: 5 ½ miles. Map. OS Landranger 164 Oxford and surrounding area (GR 389994).

Beyond Longworth and Harrowdown Hill the walk follows the bank of the upper Thames for several miles. It leaves the river at Duxford, a pretty spot, and heads for Hinton Waldrist where the striking manor house stands on the site of a Norman castle built to defend the river crossing at Duxford. The late MP Airey Neave lived here and the church contains a window in his memory.

There are splendid views over the Thames valley from this high ground. It is not too long before you return to Longworth. The last few hundred yards of the walk provide an opportunity to look at the village in more detail.

The Walk

From the car park turn right and head north out of the village. Pass Sunnymeade House and New Barn and continue along the lane. Avoid a left-hand footpath. Soon the lane drops down gently between banks. Pass Glebe Cottage on the right. At the junction of tracks bear left for a few yards, then right at the entrance to Tucks Mead. The sign here tells you that the Thames is ¾ mile.

Follow the track between trees and hedgerows. Soon it begins a gradual ascent towards the trees of Harrowdown Hill where there are striking views over to the countryside around Appleton and

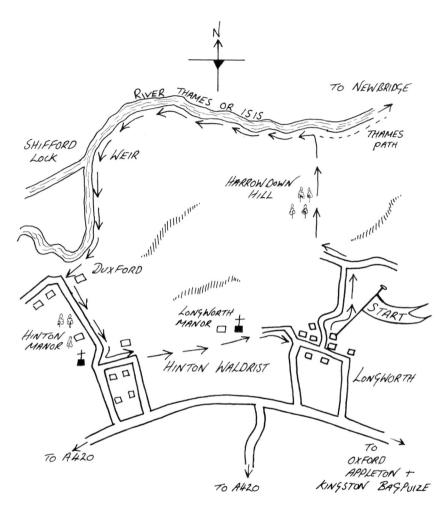

Northmoor, two Oxfordshire villages either side of the Thames. The track descends the hill and narrows to a path. Shortly it emerges from the hedgerows, at the corner of a field. Continue ahead along the signposted path, keeping the hedge on your left. In the corner drop down between banks of undergrowth to another waymarker. Go over the stile and then go straight on to join the Thames river bank. If you have time to spare you may like to head east along the river to the Rose Revived Inn at Newbridge, about 1 mile away. Then return to this point and continue the main walk.

In a few moments you reach a wooden kissing-gate. Once through it continue along the river bank. The infant Thames here is a far cry from the bustling river activity, colourful tradition and stately buildings which so characterise its Englishness downstream at Henley, Marlow, Windsor and Maidenhead. With its peaceful, unpopulated surroundings and ragged, unkempt banks, you could be forgiven for thinking this was an entirely different river.

But the Thames it most certainly is, and not that far from its source near Lechlade. Our walk follows the river bank for over 2 miles, cutting through lazy meadows and fields of cattle. The river is quite narrow at this point, snaking through the flat countryside. Where the path is hidden by undergrowth and difficult to negotiate, step over to the field edge a few feet away and follow the boundary instead. The trees of Harrowdown Hill are visible on the southerly horizon. Swans can often be glimpsed along this stretch of the Thames.

Go through another kissing-gate and pass between some willow trees. Cross a double stile and footbridge and continue. Go over another stile, still following the river bank. Fishermen may occasionally be seen amid the reeds and river plants. Cross a wooden footbridge and pass a 'private fishing' sign. Over on the right bank is the tiny isolated community of Shifford. The church stands out clearly amid the meadows. Evidence of old earthworks indicates that Shifford was a place of some importance. According to some sources, Alfred was supposed to have conducted one of the earliest English parliaments here.

Just beyond Shifford you will see the arm of Great Brook. Here the river begins to head south to the weir at Shifford Lock. The sound of rushing water is audible for some time as you approach it through the fields. Then suddenly, between banks of nettles and reeds, it is seen – the foaming cauldron of water racing over the weir. Continue along the river bank. Cattle may be seen on the opposite bank, drinking from the river. Follow the path through a strip of undergrowth and foliage and then into a tunnel of trees. Underfoot it can be a bit muddy and slippery in places.

When you emerge from the trees there are good views ahead of the buildings at Duxford. Down below, between the trees, a charming vista reveals a pretty ford which you reach at the foot of a flight of steps. At the fork take the left turning and follow the clear path between trees and banks of undergrowth. On reaching several thatched cottages at Duxford, bear left and walk along the lane. Pass some farm buildings.

The road ascends beside lines of trees and then swings right to become enclosed by manorial stone walls. Note the entrance to Hinton Manor on the right, followed by the church. Opposite the church gate take the lane between stone walls. Pass the entrance to The Grange. When the lane bends right continue ahead along a straight bridleway (Longworth 1 mile). There are striking views over the river valley at this point. Follow the path and soon there is a delightful view of the church at Longworth. Pass alongside a paddock and in the distance is Harrowdown Hill. Veer right and then left to join a drive running alongside various barns and stables belonging to Longworth Manor. The house soon comes into view on the left. Walk along the main drive between lines of tall beech trees and soon you reach the road by the entrance to the church. Go down the lane and through the village of Longworth. At the junction bear left by Rose Cottage. There is an old red telephone box in the garden. Follow the road between various houses and cottages and then turn left at the letter-box into Tucks Lane. The inn is on the right after a few yards.

19 **Sunningwell**
The Flowing Well Inn

Sunningwell means spring or well of the Sunnigas – the name given to a group of Anglo-Saxon settlers whose territory this was. The village is known for having a church with a curious, seven-sided porch which is the only one of its kind in Europe, according to locals. Roger Bacon, the famous 13th century scientist, used the tower to make astronomical observations.

Originally the village rectory, the Flowing Well has been a public house since about 1950. It is a large roomy place with an emphasis on food, which is served every day both at lunchtime and in the evening. Inside there are two bars and lots of photographs of rural scenes.

Real ales include Original and several guest beers. Other drinks include Stella Artois and Fosters, Guinness and Strongbow draught cider. On Sunday there is a choice of traditional roasts, and during the rest of the week the menu includes a selection of starters, such as soup of the day, prawn cocktail and crispy coated Cajun mushrooms. Main courses range from steaks to a large mixed grill. Cod, plaice, salmon steaks, scampi and half roast chicken are also available. There are sandwiches, ploughman's – ham, cheese and beef – various basket meals, jacket potatoes, baguettes, doorstep sandwiches and different

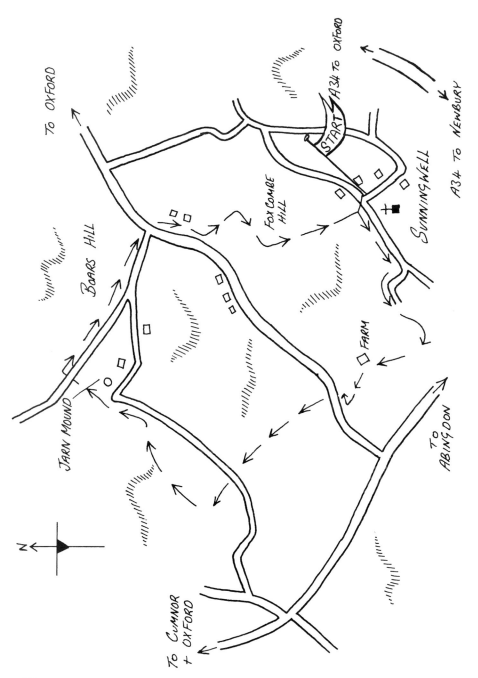

TO OXFORD

A34 TO OXFORD

START

A34 TO NEWBURY

BOARS HILL

FOX COMBE HILL

SUNNINGWELL

A34 TO NEWBURY

FARM

JARN MOUND

N

TO ABINGDON

TO CUMNOR + OXFORD

82

flavoured 'hot melts'. There is a choice of vegetarian dishes, as well as a selection of desserts.

Obedient dogs are allowed in the public bar please, well-behaved children in the eating area. Outside is an extensive and most attractive landscaped garden with many shrubs and neat, well-trimmed borders. Look out for the well along one side of the garden. It is preferable to book at weekends.

Telephone: 01865 735846.

How to get there: From the south follow the A34 and take the turning signposted Oxford ring road. Bear left at the roundabout (signposted Boars Hill). At the fork veer right towards Boars Hill and then turn left for Bayworth and Sunningwell. The inn is in the village centre, near the church.

Parking: There is a car park at the front of the inn. Sunningwell has some spaces suitable for parking a car.

Length of the walk: 4¼ miles. Map: OS Landranger 164 Oxford and surrounding area (GR 497006).

The walk heads across country to reach Matthew Arnold's Field. The Victorian poet found this spot inspired him in his work – particularly 'Thyrsis' and 'The Scholar Gipsy'. Adjacent is Jarn Mound, a 50ft high artificial mound raised in 1931 by Sir Arthur Evans, the great archaeologist, to extend and improve the view. From the high ground there are glimpses of Arnold's 'sweet city with her dreaming spires'. Between the trees the views stretch beyond Oxford to the Cherwell valley, Shotover Hill, the Chilterns and the Wittenham Clumps. Near the foot of the mound is a boulder with a plaque indicating Sir Arthur's love of antiquity, nature, freedom and youth.

The Walk

On leaving the inn car park, turn left and follow the road. Pass the road to Radley and Oxford and take the lane signposted Wootton and Abingdon. Walk through the village of Sunningwell, passing the parish church of St Leonard on the left and a red telephone box on the right. Note also the village pond.

As the road veers left turn right (signposted 'Dark Lane, the school and bridle-path'). Follow the bridleway as it bends to the left, where there are some houses. The school is on the right. At the next bend swing left and follow the track. Soon it runs along the edge of a field. The bridleway bends round to the right and here there are good views over to the right towards the wooded country around Foxcombe Hill and Boars Hill. Keep the fence on your right and continue into the next field. A group of farm buildings comes into view now. When you draw level with the buildings turn right and follow a grassy path towards them.

Keep to the left of the buildings and barns and look for a drive cutting across the fields to the road. Walk along the edge of the drive and at the road bear right. Look for a waymarker post on the left just beyond the right-hand bend in the road. Take the path (signposted Old Boars Hill) and follow it across the open fields. Go through a gap in the boundary hedge and continue towards a white house ahead. On reaching the house, cross a stile and go out to the road. Take the track opposite (signposted Cumnor).

Follow the track and then at the corrugated barn take the path running along the side of the building. Cross several more stiles and then cross the field to the far boundary. Aim for the stiles in the right-hand corner and enter the next field. Walk ahead with the boundary hedge on your left. Look for a stile in the next fence; continue ahead towards the field corner. Take the first of two stiles in the fence and cross into the paddock on your left. Make for the top right-hand corner of the field, go over another stile and cross a grassy path between trees and hedgerows.

Keep to the track as it cuts between houses and cottages. Pass Collyers and continue to the road. Turn left and pass Barn Cottage. When the lane bends right continue ahead by Broom Close, the name of a house. Follow the track and soon you reach a junction by Matthew Arnold's Field, bought for the Oxford Preservation Trust through public subscription from both sides of the Atlantic. The field, fringed by woodland, is one of the scenic delights of this walk. Turn right for a few yards and then left through a kissing-gate to reach the steps to Jarn Mound, 530 ft above sea level. Descending the flight of steps go through the gate at the bottom of the steps, bear right and follow the path to the road, turning right.

At the next junction go straight on (Berkeley Road). This is Boars Hill. Pass the entrance to Foxcombe Hall (part of the Open University) on the right. On the left now are glimpses, beyond the fields and between the trees, of Oxford's spires. The land here is owned by the Oxford Preservation Trust. At the next junction turn right and follow the pavement. Follow the road round the right-hand curve. On reaching a bus stop cross over to a waymarked drive (signposted Sunningwell).

Follow the drive and after a few hundred yards it bends right. Pass the entrance to Withy Copse and continue as the drive bends left. Pass a turning on the right and a letter-box. The drive cuts between private residences situated in extensive wooded grounds. Soon the drive bears right at the entrance to Gayhurst. Go through a wooden kissing-gate and down the grassy path towards the village of Sunningwell. At the next field boundary go through another kissing-gate and out to the road. Opposite you is the parish church of St Leonard. Turn left and return to the inn, which is located on the right at the next junction.

20 Fernham
The Woodman Inn

The Woodman is an ancient inn dating back 400 years to the 15th century. The history of this delightful and popular pub is documented inside. The Manor of Shrivenham held lands in the Manor of Fernham and according to the records there was a beer house on this site, selling locally brewed beer. The inn has been known as the Woodman for about 150 years, its earliest-recorded landlord was William King in 1840. The longest-serving landlord was James Warner, who ran the Woodman for 56 years, between 1915 and 1971. Sadly, many of the original records of the quarter sessions, containing the licensing grants, were lost in a fire at Reading in 1703.

The interior of the pub comprises a rambling bar area full of beams and fascinating artefacts. There are clay pipes to see and smoke, coach horns, tables made from old casks and various black and white photographs of village scenes and local characters. There is a big log fire in the bar, warm and cosy on a cold winter's day, an adjacent dining area and a converted barn used as a banqueting hall. The emphasis here is on good food and beer from the wood, and real ales include Archers, Morland Original and Theakston Old Peculier. There is also Scrumpy Jack cider, Guinness and Carlsberg lager. The menu boasts various starters – garlic mushrooms, prawn cocktail, home-made soup and pâté among them. Main courses include deep fried haddock and chips, chicken breast, home cooked gammon, breaded scampi, sirloin steak, home-made Woodman pie, mushroom stroganoff, noisettes of lamb, Penne pasta with a ratatouille sauce, and kangaroo. There is a selection of baguettes and a daily chef's specials board, plus a choice of potatoes and vegetables or chips and salads with many of the dishes on the menu. Children and dogs are welcome; there is a beer garden outside.

Telephone: 01367 820643.

How to get there: Follow the A417 between Wantage and Faringdon and then join the B4508 for Shellingford and Fernham. The inn is on the left.

Parking: There is a car park at the pub, and there may be room to park elsewhere in Fernham.

Length of the walk: 2 ¾ miles. Map: OS Landranger 174 Newbury and Wantage (GR 293918).

This quite short walk explores an area of delightful countryside in the Vale of the White Horse. On the route, you come across hidden pockets of woodland and glimpses of distant hills. The return leg offers some of the best views.

The Walk

From the car park turn right and walk down to the right-hand bend. At this point leave the main road and go into Chapel Lane. Pass some semi-detached houses on the left and continue along the lane (signposted 'circular walk'). When it bends right, go forward, across the stile and into the field. Note the wooded hillside over on your left. Walk across the field keeping to the right-hand boundary. Go through a gate into the next field. Veer slightly left towards the gate in the next boundary and then aim half-left to reach the next gate in the far boundary. Glancing back at this stage it is possible to pinpoint one or two outstanding features in this corner of Oxfordshire. To the south, beyond the houses of Fernham, lies the spectacular Vale of the White Horse.

On reaching a bridleway turn left and walk along between hedges and rows of beech trees. Pheasants may be seen scurrying about nervously in the surrounding woods, confused by the sound of your approaching footsteps. Soon a field comes into view on the right, prettily enclosed by trees. Follow the bridleway as it continues alongside the field. There are also glimpses of fields beyond the trees on the left. Here you will see fir and silver birch trees, as well as

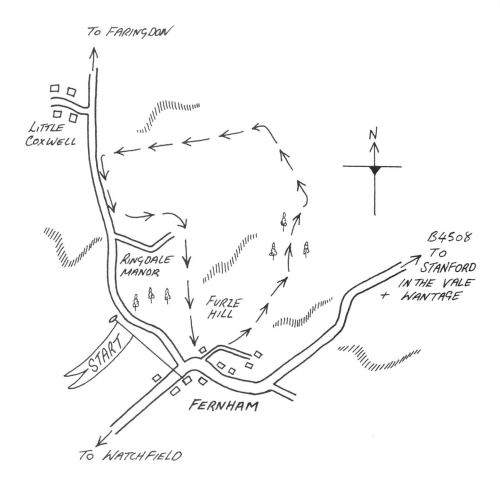

clumps of brambles amid the undergrowth.

The path descends between lines of trees and curves left. Avoid a
turning on the right and continue for a few yards to a field edge. Keep
right at the fork and follow the sandy bridleway. Fields and banks of
scrub line the route. Begin a gentle ascent; behind you are good views
over the lines of fir trees towards the distant Vale of the White Horse.
When the path reaches the level ground you will see a waymarker post
up ahead. In front of you on the horizon are the wooded slopes of
Badbury Hill. The hill rises to 500 ft and is the site of an Iron Age hill
fort.

On reaching the footpath sign bear left and walk along the field
edge. Pass into the next field, under some power lines and progress

towards the houses of Little Coxwell. The A420 road is visible over to the right as you look toward Faringdon. The path becomes a grassy track and descends towards the road at Gorse Farm. Go out to the road and bear left. Follow the road away from Little Coxwell and as it begins to head up the slope, swing left on to a signposted bridleway. Follow the track round to the right and alongside rows of fir trees.

At the next junction of paths turn right (signposted 'circular walk'). Follow the path between fields and strips of woodland. Pass several field gates on the left and the entrance to Ringdale Manor on the right. Continue on the straight path. Between the trees and in various gateways there are glorious vistas over to the ridge of hills surrounding the Vale of the White Horse. At one point, when the trees thin to be replaced by hedgerows, there is a particularly striking view of the downland slopes rising up to meet the sky.

The path descends quite steeply between rolling fields and trees. Cross a stile into a field and walk ahead with the boundary on your left. Cross a second stile in the next boundary, follow a path alongside a productive vegetable garden and then join a drive. At the road turn right and return to the inn.

㉑ Letcombe Regis
The Greyhound

Letcombe Regis is synonymous with racehorse training and it is not uncommon to see strings of horses heading along the winding streets of the village, on their way to exercise on the nearby downs. The growing of watercress in the Letcombe Brook also helped to put Letcombe Regis on the map.

The Greyhound has a fascinating history. The last reading of the Riot Act in England took place on the steps of the pub early in the 20th century, apparently provoked by a dispute involving local stable lads. The Greyhound dates back to the late 17th century and was originally an inn and several small cottages. The building became the pub you see today during the Victorian era. At present, there are two bars and a dining area but the new landlord plans to create a new restaurant and transform the menu. Popular with walkers on the nearby Ridgeway, the inn also draws visitors touring the Vale of the White Horse by car. Sandwiches, soup, baguettes and baked potatoes will appeal to those who enjoy a light snack, while spaghetti bolognaise, beef stroganoff, fish and a range of steaks are likely to catch the attention of anyone looking for something a bit more substantial. Food is available every day, there is also a summer barbecue and a traditional Sunday roast at certain times of the year. Real ales include Morland Original and a guest beer, while Fosters and Kronenbourg are among the lagers. For the cider drinker there is Strongbow on draught. The Greyhound also offers accommodation. There are 5 rooms – 2 doubles, 2 singles and 1 twin. The famous throwing game, Aunt Sally, is played in the garden; there is also a pets' corner and a children's playing area.

Telephone: 01235 770905.

How to get there: From the centre of Wantage take the B4507 west towards Shrivenham. The turning for Letcombe Regis is on the left. The Greyhound is on the left in the main street.

Parking: There is a car park at the pub, and it is possible to park in the vicinity of the inn or elsewhere in the village.

Length of the walk: 3½ miles. Map: OS Landranger 174 Newbury and Wantage (GR 381865).

The spectacular Vale of the White Horse is viewed during this superb downland walk. Beginning in Letcombe Regis, the route heads immediately for the ridge of the Downs, passing alongside the Iron Age fort known as Segsbury Camp. Beyond this site the walk briefly joins the Ridgeway before heading north to the village of Letcombe Bassett. The last mile is along a delightful path running above the Letcombe brook.

The Walk

Emerging from the inn, turn left and walk along the village street to the church. Bear left (signposted 'Downs') and follow the road to the edge of Letcombe Regis. Head south along Warborough Road. Pass an assortment of houses and cottages followed by the buildings of Warborough Farm. Follow the road towards the ridge of the Downs. The road climbs now, becoming progressively steeper as you make your way towards the Ridgeway and the summit of the Downs. Over to your right is the Sparsholt radio transmitter. The road ascends in dramatic fashion, cutting between trees and hedgerows. Looking back at intervals reveals good views over to Letcombe Regis with the downland slopes rising above the village.

When the road levels out on the higher ground, continue between the ramparts of Segsbury Camp. This is the site of an Iron Age hill fort and according to the information board 'is similar in size and importance to the forts at Uffington and Barbury'. The site consists of more than 26 acres and is located on land owned by a local farmer who has recently agreed to enter his land into the Countryside Stewardship scheme. This involves the fort reverting to sheep pasture.

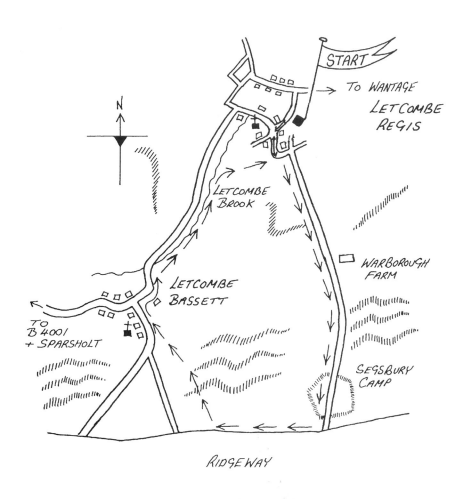

START

TO WANTAGE

LETCOMBE
REGIS

N

LETCOMBE
BROOK

WARBOROUGH
FARM

LETCOMBE
BASSETT

TO
B 4001
+ SPARSHOLT

SEGSBURY
CAMP

RIDGEWAY

Scrub will be cleared by local volunteers and the original layout of the camp will become evident. Any loss of nesting sites and wildlife habitats will be recovered by the planting of woodland and scrub elsewhere on the farmer's land. Iron Age pottery has been discovered at Segsbury Camp and a Saxon burial site was unearthed in the 19th century. Walk along to the junction with the Ridgeway and turn right to join the famous and historic route – one of Britain's foremost national trails and extending for 85 miles between Avebury in Wiltshire and Ivinghoe Beacon in Buckinghamshire.

Follow the Ridgeway in a westerly direction. The track is wide along this stretch, as it is for much of the entire route. The movement of travellers from side to side down the years has resulted in this ancient road becoming as broad as a main road. Pass a waymarked path on the left. Soon a waymarked path (signposted Letcombe Bassett) comes into view on the right. Take the path and follow down the grassy slopes. In front of you is a magnificent downland panorama; the buildings of Letcombe Bassett are visible down below amid the trees.

Head for a stile in the next boundary and then over several more stiles, all the time keeping the woodland on your right. The field path drops down steeply into a dip and then rises again. Avoid a path on the right leading into the trees, go over another stile and then along the field edge, with the fence on your left. Cross another stile and go out to the road.

Turn right and walk down into Letcombe Bassett. Thomas Hardy based the village of Cresscombe on this village in his novel *Jude the Obscure*. Note the church visible over to the left as you enter the village. At the junction swing right towards Wantage and Letcombe Regis. Pass Downs House, with its collection of thatched buildings and barns, and when the road bends sharp left by some cottages go straight on to join a path (signposted 'Letcombe Regis 1 mile'). Follow the path; the road is visible down below running parallel to our route. The Letcombe brook can be seen down amid the trees, dashing prettily through the wooded gorge. Several picturesque cottages may also be glimpsed along this stretch. This is one of the most attractive sections of the entire walk, as the route follows sheltered paths enclosed by trees and foliage with glimpses of spectacular downland in the distance. In autumn the trees are a dazzling blaze of colour.

Eventually the path veers away to the right at a gate. One final glance down towards the water reveals a charming picture. In the distance, on the horizon, is the dramatic outline of Hackpen Hill and the Devil's Punchbowl. Soon the houses of Letcombe Regis come into view. Bear to the left and join a grassy ride. Turn right at a stile and footpath sign and follow the path between trees to the road. Turn left, then right by the church and walk back to the Greyhound.

22 East Hendred
The Wheatsheaf

East Hendred is a charming village full of picturesque thatched and timber-framed cottages. Situated below the Ridgeway, it was once well known as a centre for cloth.

The Wheatsheaf is a 300-year-old building with lots of olde worlde charm. It became a Morland pub in the 1920s. Inside, there are low ceilings, beams and horse brasses. Real ales include Morland Bitter, Ruddles County and Old Speckled Hen. There are also Scrumpy Jack cider and Foster's lager. Among the bar snacks are various sandwiches and ploughman's, as well as a steak roll. Among the home-made daily specials you may find authentic Indian curry, breaded scampi, gammon steak and chips, chilli con carne, breaded plaice. There is also a range of jacket potatoes – chilli, curry, prawn cocktail, cheese and baked beans among them. The main menu includes several starters, such as prawn and mushrooms, soup of the day and avocado vinaigrette, while among the main courses are lamb steak marinade, fresh Scottish salmon and steak chasseur. From the grill you can choose 8 oz sirloin and Wheatsheaf mixed grill. There are several vegetarian dishes, sweets, including hot chocolate fudge cake, Danish freeze cake and banana surprise, and on Sunday a traditional lunch.

94

Both children and dogs are welcome. At the rear is a beer garden with a play area.
Telephone: 01235 833229.

How to get there: From the A34 take the A417 and follow it towards Wantage. Turn left (signposted East Hendred village); at the war memorial turn sharp right into Chapel Square and the inn is on the right.

Parking: There is room to park at the pub and in the village.

Length of the walk: 4½ miles. Map: OS Landranger 174 Newbury and Wantage (GR 461888).

Crossing the pretty Ginge brook, the walk makes for the village of Ardington, built as part of an 18,000-acre country estate established by Baron Wantage VC in the 19th century. A reporter from the Daily News *wrote of the estate in 1891: 'It is a little self-contained world in which nobody is idle, nobody is in absolute want, in which there is no hunger or squalor.' Baron Wantage, who fought in the Crimean War, lived at Ardington House, which is seen on the route of the walk.*

The Walk
On leaving the inn turn left, then right at the junction. Pass the 13th century parish church and Church Street and continue along Newbury Road. Bear right into Horn Lane and pass a row of terraced cottages. Continue ahead to join The Lynch and follow the bridleway between fields.

In time you reach a track. Go straight ahead and over a stile on to a footpath. Cross the field to reach the road and in front of you now is 14th century Holy Trinity church. Its setting is truly delightful: by the pleasant meadows of the Ginge brook. Walk past the church and across the meadows. On this stretch you cross a stile, then a stone and brick footbridge over the tumbling Ginge brook. Follow the path through some trees and head out across the fields. Soon you pass alongside the buildings of a pig farm. Join a firm track and continue ahead.

At the next junction proceed ahead on a grassy path; there is a sign here – Ardington and Lockinge parishes. Pass a gate to a fishery and some sluice gates on the right. Just beyond the lake is the southerly façade of Ardington House, an elegant 18th century mansion.

Turn right at the road and make for the centre of Ardington. The craft complex, comprising various craft shops and potteries converted from old stables and farm buildings, is to the west of the famous estate village.

95

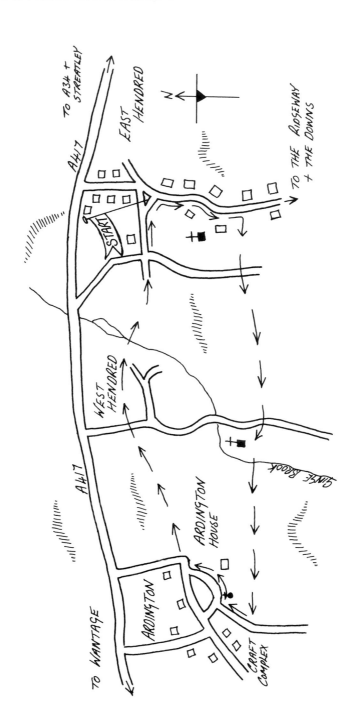

Bear right and pass the church and the inn. Note also the entrance to Ardington House; the sign here says: '1720, Historic Houses Association'.

At the next junction turn right opposite Ardington Butchery. When the road bends left go straight on along a lane and then veer left at Jubilee Cottages. Pass some houses, go through a belt of woodland and then cross three small fields interposed with strips of woodland before swinging half-left across the field to a stile. In the next field keep to the right-hand edge; cross a grass track and go on along a field path towards the houses of West Hendred. At the road turn right for a short distance, then left between houses.

Cross a stile, then a field to reach a thatched cottage. Pass through some double gates, then bear left over a stile. There are farm buildings on the right at this stage. Cross another stile in the next corner; go across the field to a footbridge where you recross the Ginge brook. Cross another footbridge and then join a drive, following it to a bungalow. Take the path alongside the gate and soon you reach the road.

Turn right and at the next junction join Orchard Lane. Follow it to Orchard Stables and then bear right into Chapel Square. The Wheatsheaf inn is on the left.

23 Aston Tirrold
The Chequers

Aston Tirrold is a pretty village of thatched cottages and half-timbered houses, so close to its neighbour Aston Upthorpe that it is difficult to distinguish between the two communities.

The Chequers is situated at the heart of this Oxfordshire racing village, and not surprisingly the inn is popular with trainers and jockeys. It is a Georgian, Grade II listed building comprising a main lounge bar and games area, where you can play pool and darts. Children and dogs are welcome and there is a large garden.

The lounge bar has brick pillars, horse brasses, panelled walls and various prints of horses, dogs and partridge and grouse shooting scenes. Those who love nostalgia will appreciate the print of an old advertisement for 'Virginia Number Seven' cigarettes. The advert depicts a hunting scene and a huntsman smoking a cigarette. The caption reads: 'The trees and hedges glowing brown against the green acres – and the violent glitter of scarlet flickering in and out of view. The peaceful glory of an awakening November morning – and the little friendly groan of leather rubbing leather. The anticipation of vigorous hours to come – and the stolen pleasure of a few lazy minutes. And for perfection, one thing more – Number Seven.'

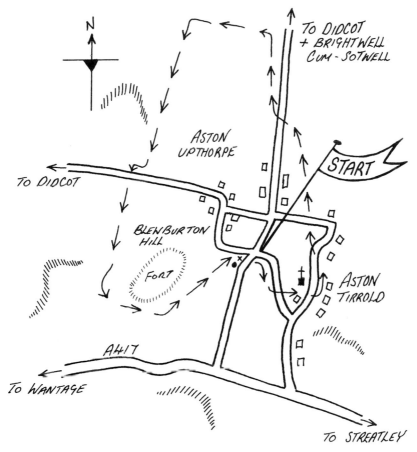

The extensive menu includes soup of the day, garlic mushrooms and prawn cocktail; among the grills are 8 oz rump steak, gammon steak and mixed grill. Other dishes include braised pork in orange and ginger and chicken in a smoked oyster and cream sauce. There are also ploughman's, baguettes, filled rolls, soup and salads, as well as a traditional Sunday roast. Vegetarians are catered for too, and desserts include spotted dick, treacle tart and bread and butter pudding. Among the real ales are Marston's Pedigree, Tetley and Morland Old Speckled Hen, with Lowenbrau lager, Guinness and Strongbow cider providing other drinks.

Telephone: 01235 851272.

How to get there: Join the A417 south of Abingdon and follow it in an easterly direction through Upton and Blewbury. The turning for Aston Tirrold is on the left. The Chequers is on the right in the village centre.

Parking: There is a pub car park where you can leave your car whilst out walking. Some alternative spaces can be found in the village.

Length of the walk: 3 miles. Map: OS Landranger 174 Newbury and Wantage (GR 554862).

A wide expanse of Oxfordshire is viewed on this windswept walk. Towards the end the route reaches Blewburton Hill, a famous local landmark and once the site of an Iron Age fort. Nearby are the Downs and the Ridgeway.

The Walk

From the inn car park turn left into Baker Street (signposted Reading) and then follow the road round to the right. Just beyond a telephone box bear left to join a path lined by hedgerows and trees. Follow the path through the churchyard and at the road turn left. When the road veers to the right, go straight on along a path between hedges. On reaching the road cross over and continue along the path. Pass over a concrete farm track and then cross the field, keeping to the right of a row of silos.

Make for a stile in the far boundary, cross a farm track into the next field and continue. Aim for the stile in the far corner of the field and then emerge on to the road. Turn right and follow the road, noting the chimneys of Didcot Power Station in the distance. There is a line of beech trees on your immediate right. Pass a row of bungalows on the right and then take a bridleway on the left. There are good southerly views of the Downs at this point.

On reaching a junction of paths bear left through a wooden kissing-gate and follow a clear grassy path running alongside some paddocks. Eventually you join a track; follow it to the road and then swing right. After a few yards turn left to cross a stile and skirt the field. There are impressive views here over open, exposed country.

Look out for a stile after several minutes; it will be found in the left-hand boundary fence. Cross the stile, then bear immediately right and walk along the lower flank of Blewburton Hill. The hill is 300 ft high and contains some strip lynchets and an extensive Iron Age fort. Follow the path along the chalky slopes and then reach a bridleway. Turn left and follow the track until you reach a stile on the left. Cross it and then swing right. Follow the grassy path and go through a kissing-gate. Descend some shallow steps and join a track running to the road. Turn right, noting All Saints church at this point, and follow the lane beside a pretty, timber-framed house. The Chequers comes into view now, just a few yards ahead of you at the junction.

24 Hailey, near Ipsden
The King William IV

Originally this listed building was a coaching inn on the road to Wallingford. The horses were changed here and stabled at the rear. Until recently the King William was a simple, straightforward drinkers' local, famous in the area for its collection of old farm implements, vintage tractors, horsedrawn ploughs and many other relics from a past farming age. The new landlord aims to expand the choice of food to include everything from baguettes to steak, while at the same time retaining many of the charming features for which the pub is so well known. A traditional Sunday roast is one of the inn's more popular attractions. The King William's classic Chilterns setting makes the pub an obvious watering hole for walkers exploring this glorious corner of Oxfordshire. Roaring log fires give the inn a cosy feel in winter and many visitors favour the King William for its splendid unspoilt views.

Beer is tapped from casks behind the bar and includes Brakspear Pale Ale, Special and Old Ale. Bulmers draught cider is also available, as are Heineken and Stella Artois lagers. Children are welcome in the adjoining eating areas, at lunchtime only. Dogs on a lead are permitted inside. The pub is open all day in summer.

Telephone: 01491 681845.

How to get there: From Wallingford head south on the A4074 towards Woodcote. Turn left (signposted Ipsden, Well Place and Stoke Row). At the crossroads turn left, then right for Hailey. The inn is on the left.

Parking: The car park at the inn is the best place to leave a vehicle. There are very few spaces in the nearby roads and lanes.

Length of the walk: 3½ miles. Map: OS Landranger 175 Reading, Windsor and surrounding area (GR 642858).

There are gorgeous views over the rolling wooded Chilterns on this walk. On the return leg there is an opportunity to visit Well Place Zoo.

The Walk
Leave the pub by turning left. Follow the lane between hedgerows and trees. Pass a house and some outbuildings on the right; now the lane becomes rougher underfoot. There are glorious views here over the wooded Chiltern country of south-east Oxfordshire. Pass a bridleway on the right and continue along the track.

Soon the route begins a gentle climb as you approach Bixmoor Wood. A track runs in from the left along this stretch. Continue through the woodland, following the track as it twists and bends between the trees and clearings. Pass a gate on the left with a notice which reads 'Private woodland – no public right of way'. Beyond the entrance to Fludgers Wood, an isolated house set amid the hills and woods, the track bends left and then reaches some cottages. Turn right, over a stile, into the field. Go down the field, veering a little to the right towards the stile in the far boundary. Enter the woodland and follow the path through the trees. Over to the right you should catch glimpses of a large white house – this is Handsmooth. Cross over a muddy track and continue down through the woodland. The views over rolling fields and woods are particularly striking.

The path drops down between banks of undergrowth before reaching a bridleway. Turn right and follow it through the trees to reach some timber and corrugated farm buildings. Continue beyond the buildings, still following the bridleway. Pass Lower Handsmooth Farm and a footpath on the left. At the road junction you have a choice. To visit Well Place Zoo (open every day 10 am to 5 pm Easter to September, weekends only October to March – if the weather is suitable) carry on along the road signposted North Stoke and Crowmarsh. The zoo entrance is on the right.

The main walk bears left at the junction (signposted to Stoke Row and Nuffield). Follow the lane between trees and banks; as it bends left take the first of two waymarked footpaths on the right. Go over a stile

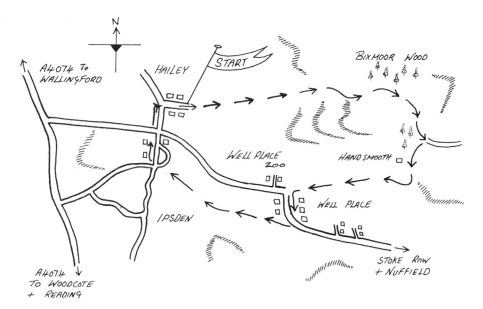

and into the field. Walk ahead with a hedge on the left and views over to Well Place Zoo and the wooded hill country of the Chilterns. The middle stages of this walk, the area of countryside around Handsmooth, can be seen from here.

Aim for the field corner and cross a dilapidated stile. Follow a narrow enclosed path between trees and hedges. Soon the path bends right and graduates to a grassy ride running down to the road. As it does so turn left by a sign 'horses keep left'. Follow the path between the vast, prairie-like fields; there is a fence on the right and a hedgerow on the left. Eventually the path runs alongside the gardens of private houses on the right.

At the road turn right (signposted to Ipsden church, Well Place and Hailey). Pass Crabtree Corner and continue to the junction. Go straight across towards Hailey. Turn right after several hundred yards and walk along the lane back to the inn.

25 Satwell
The Lamb

The Lamb is one of many traditional country inns to be found in this south-east corner of Oxfordshire. The building, one of the oldest in the area, is reputed to date back to the 16th century and was originally a one up, one down farm worker's cottage. The Lamb has been a public house for at least 200 years.

The interior comprises a cosy, beamed main bar with a big fireplace and an adjacent eating area. There is also a newly opened first floor, non-smoking restaurant. Food is served daily, at both sessions; the choice of meals is varied and comprehensive with a popular range of light bites and filled baguettes – cheee, ham, hot sausage, bacon, tuna, prawn and steak. The ploughman's include Cheddar, Brie and red Leicester, and starters or light snacks range from French onion soup to duck and port pâté. Among the fish dishes are scampi and breaded plaice. Vegetarians are catered for with cashew-nut paella and avocado and corn bake. From the grill you can choose 8 oz rump steak, mixed grill, lamb tikka steak and cajun chicken. Desserts include banana split, crème caramel, jam roly-poly and spotted dick. There is also a blackboard for daily specials and a well-priced children's menu.

Real ales include Brakspear Special Bitter and OBJ, backed up by

Scrumpy Jack draught cider, Murphy's and Stella Artois and Heineken lagers. Well-behaved children and dogs are welcome; outside is a beer garden with a play area. Note the sign: 'Horses welcome – shovel available'! Large groups are requested to book.
Telephone: 01491 628482.

How to get there: From Nettlebed head south on the B481 and then swing left at the sign to Shepherd's Green. The inn is on the right after a short distance.

Parking: There is a car park at the Lamb. Space elsewhere is rather restricted.

Length of the walk: 4 miles. Map: OS Landranger 175 Reading, Windsor and surrounding area (GR 706834).

The rich beauty of the Chiltern beechwoods plays a key role in this delightful and varied walk which is probably best appreciated in autumn or spring. The route cuts through the woods to reach Greys Court.

The Walk

From the Lamb's car park turn left and walk along the lane. At the road junction turn right to join a waymarked woodland path. The path, muddy in places, keeps quite close to the edge of the trees. Disregard the stile in the right-hand boundary fence and keep on the main path. Gradually it curves to the left as you approach the end of the trees; in a few moments you reach the single-track road.

Turn right and follow the lane, passing a bridleway at one point. Fields and bursts of woodland make up the attractive scene either side of the lane. Pass the entrance to Rocky Lane Farm on the left and then a pond on the right where there is also a footpath to Shepherd's Green. Beyond several more paths and the entrance to Rose Farm, the lane begins to descend beneath overhanging trees. When it curves right join a bridleway and follow it down through the trees. A pretty tree-fringed field comes into view on the left, on the right is dense woodland.

Cross a muddy bridleway and go through a gate. Follow the path ahead, noting the National Trust sign, 'Vermin control is carried out in these woods. Please keep your dogs under strict close control'. Progress up the steep bank, following the white arrows on the trees. Glancing back offers a glorious vista over thickly afforested Oxfordshire countryside. Continue ahead through the lovely Chiltern beechwoods, allowing the white waymarkers to guide you between the trees. As you approach the woodland edge begin to veer over to

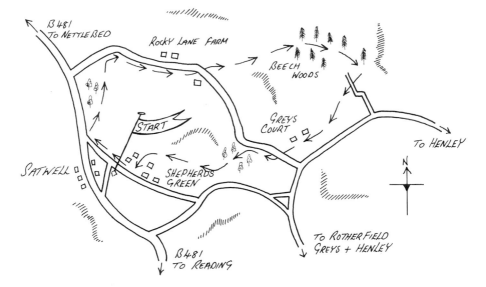

the left, still following the arrows. On the right are glimpses of open farmland through the lines of trees.

Pass a footpath on the left. There are some buildings away to the left. Up ahead, a little to the left, you will see a field corner edging into view. As you approach it look for the junction of paths defined by yellow and white arrows on one of the trees. Turn right, follow the yellow arrows and head for the woodland edge where you will see a stile. Cross the field, keeping some houses to the right of you. Pass under some telegraph wires, cross several stiles with a lane in between and aim for the next field boundary.

Pass into the next field and cross it to the woodland on the far side. Join a waymarked woodland path and follow it as it bends round to the left beneath some beech trees. There is a pond on the right and some farm buildings are on the left. Go through a wooden gate, turn right and follow a grassy track. Pass over a footbridge and continue down to a stile. Enter the parkland of Greys Court and go up the slope to the next stile. There is a sign here requesting that dogs be kept on a lead due to sheep grazing.

Cross the parkland and on reaching the drive by the admission kiosk, turn right. Walk along the drive and pass the entrance to the main house and tower on the right. Originally a fortified manor house, the present gabled brick and flint house is Elizabethan. Greys Court includes a Tudor donkey wheel well-house and the garden contains the Archbishop's Maze, based on the theme of reconciliation. The house and garden are open to the public during the summer. For more information ring 01491 628529. Greys Court is in the care of the National Trust.

Rolling Chiltern parkland makes up the scene on the left of the house. Follow the drive down the slope to the road. Turn right and pass a footpath crossing the route of the road and then a permitted path on the right. As the road curves right take a footpath on the left. Go up to the top right corner of the field, passing under some telegraph wires. Cross another stile and join a woodland path. Further up, the path swings left and reaches yet another stile. Continue ahead through the trees, following the arrows. Go straight on at a junction of paths and at the end of the trees join a path running between trees, hedgerow and paddocks. Cross another stile and soon you join a path cutting between wire fences. There is a large house on the left. Emerge from the path at a junction of drives surrounded by the houses and cottages of Shepherd's Green. Turn left and walk along to the road. Note the red telephone box.

Bear right and follow the road. Pass Satwell Close and continue between trees and hedgerows. One or two houses can be glimpsed beyond the fields and paddocks. Pass the imposing entrance to Satwells Barton and after a few yards you reach the inn car park.

26 Nuffield
The Crown

This popular brick and flint inn, adjacent to Huntercombe Golf Club and on the route of the Ridgeway, dates back to the 17th century. Records indicate that it was a pub in 1675 – the then landlord was buried that year. Originally it was a wagoners' inn. Inside, the lounge bar has an inglenook fireplace, beams, and lots of plates and prints of flowers and country scenes. There is also a print of Willie Park, the 19th century golfing champion.

Real ales include Brakspear Special, Ordinary and various seasonal beers, while lager-drinkers can enjoy Fosters. There is a good choice of food at lunchtime and in the evening. Starters or light meals include home-made soup, chicken liver pâté, deep-fried brie and whitebait salmon mousse. Among the main meals is steak and kidney pie, one of the inn's most popular and perennial dishes. Other favourites include liver and bacon, fresh fish specials, bangers and mash with home-made sausages, steak sandwich, rack of lamb, chicken and leek pie, pasta of the day and 'Pork Hobbler'. A range of sandwiches and ploughman's are also available, and there is a traditional roast on Sunday. The Crown offers a choice of mouth-watering desserts, including chocolate chip sponge, spotted dick, and apple and blackberry almond pudding. Children are welcome at lunchtime, but not in the bar. Dogs on a lead please. It is preferable to book in advance.

Telephone: 01491 641335.

How to get there: From Wallingford follow the A4130 (formerly the A423) and the inn is on the right near Huntercombe Golf Club.

Parking: There is plenty of room to park at the inn. It is advisable to park here as the A4130 is a busy road.

Length of the walk: 4 miles. Map. OS Landranger 175 Reading, Windsor and surrounding area (GR 675876).

For the first mile or so the route of this walk coincides with the Ridgeway. It crosses the fairways of Huntercombe Golf Club to reach the church at Nuffield. This is high ground – the southern Chilterns. From here it is a short walk to the edge of Mongewell Woods, one of the delights of this varied walk. The route cuts across country for some time to reach Grim's Ditch, an ancient earthwork, just before rejoining the golf course.

The Walk

From the front door of the inn turn left and then left again at the main road. Pass a telephone box and after a few yards you reach a sign for the Ridgeway; you will see the waymarkers carrying the familiar acorn logo. Don't cross the road. Instead follow the path as it cuts between Fairway Cottage and a private garage. After a few yards you reach the edge of Huntercombe golf course. Follow the numbered white posts across the fairways. The Ridgeway runs into some woods where there are glimpses of the fairways between the trees. As you approach the clubhouse veer right to a stile and then go across the fields to a clump of trees and the church at Nuffield, which has the grave of William Morris, Viscount Nuffield, the renowned car manufacturer and benefactor.

At the road turn right and pass the church, with its flint face and shingle tower. Turn left at the Ridgeway waymarker and follow the field edge. A large white house comes into view on the left. Cross the stile in the field corner and join a path cutting through a belt of trees and holly bushes. Soon the Ridgeway ventures away to the right; disregard it and continue ahead, crossing a stile.

Keep to the path as it emerges from the woodland and cuts along the field edge. In the corner go over a rather primitive wrought-iron ladder stile and then follow the path between banks of undergrowth. A house can be seen over to the right. Cross the drive to the house, just south of

109

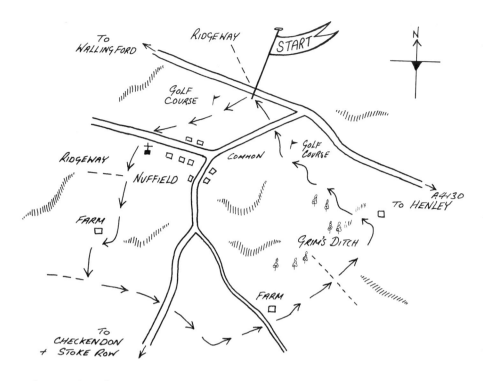

the garden fence, and then follow the right of way south across the arable field, keeping parallel to the new driveway. Bear left at the next junction and walk along to the road. Cross over and follow the bridleway towards some farm buildings. As you approach them look for a gap in the left-hand hedge and cross the stile into the field. Aim for some trees in the right-hand boundary, near a large house. Cross the stile and pass a hard tennis court on the right. At the drive bear left and follow it as it veers right. When you draw level with the house swing half-right and go over a cattle grid. Follow a track along the edge of the field, making for some farm buildings. Go over a stile in the field corner and continue towards the farm. At the junction turn right and then second left beside a timber barn. The track runs round the back of the farmhouse and its buildings and then bends to the right.

Soon a stile comes into view on the left. Cross into the field and go diagonally across it to the far corner, dropping down into the dip and then up again. There are good views here across a rich rolling landscape interspersed with trees and occasional farm buildings. Cross the stile and bear left along the bridleway. Avoid another bridleway on the left and continue ahead towards a farm. An electricity

110

substation is visible here. Turn left immediately before the farm buildings, where a sign requests you to keep dogs on a lead, and go forward with the farm on the right and a corrugated hay barn on the left.

Cross the stile in the next boundary and then make for a line of trees ahead. In this immediate area is evidence of Grim's Ditch. Go over another stile at the next gate and then veer over to the right-hand side of the field and make for another stile in the corner. You are now back at the edge of Huntercombe golf course. Cross the first fairway and then swing half-right to a red post and then go through the gap into the trees on the left. Cross the next fairway, veering a little to the right and then maintain the same direction until you reach the road. Cross the road and continue for a short distance across the fairways until you reach the Crown car park.

27 Maidensgrove
The Five Horseshoes

An extremely popular inn and well known in the locality, the Five Horseshoes dates back to the early 17th century. Then, the wives took charge of the business while the menfolk worked on the land. With a little imagination you can picture how this pub might have looked in those days. A few customers would brave it this far, but many would have been put off by its isolated position.

Today many of the inn's original features remain, including a low ceiling and plenty of beams, but now it boasts a lively, bustling atmosphere and a general air of fun and excitement. The real ales include Brakspear Special Bitter and Ordinary, as well as several guest beers. Lagers are Stella Artois and Heineken, and Guinness is also available.

The emphasis is very much on food at the Five Horseshoes and the choice is excellent and very well presented. Starters and snacks cover soup of the day, home-made pâté – chicken liver, smoked salmon and vegetarian – plus a range of ploughman's and pancakes. Main courses range from fish fillets of sole, stir-fried chicken, salmon and crab cakes, lamb cutlets and chargrilled tuna steak to wild boar sausages. Stilton soup is one of the inn's specialities, as are calf's liver and steak and kidney pie. Puddings include pecan and maple syrup tart, cheesecake and continental ice cream. A traditional Sunday roast is also available. Adjacent to the bar is the newly opened Café Shoes bistro-style restaurant, which offers striking views over the Chilterns. Starters here include grilled goats' cheese. Among the main dishes are grilled Barnsley chop and warm chicken salad. There is also the Club Room which used to be the stable and is now a dining and meeting room. Outside is a beer garden and a pretty arbour with tables and chairs and a barbecue. Dogs must be kept on a lead. Children are welcome at lunchtime in either the Café Shoes, garden roadside bar or Club Room. It is advisable to ring and book at weekends.

Telephone: 01491 641282.

How to get there: From Henley take the A4130, then join the B480 and head towards Watlington. Turn left at Stonor (signposted Maidensgrove) and follow the road through the village and beyond the commons. The inn is then on the left.

Parking: There is plenty of room to park opposite the inn. Anywhere else might be a little difficult as the inn is rather remote.

Length of the walk: 2 ¾ miles. Map: OS Landranger 175 Reading, Windsor and surrounding area (GR 711891).

The surroundings on this walk are exceptionally attractive, and the views over the Chiltern hills stunning. The walk will appeal to naturalists and country lovers, as it explores the Warburg Nature Reserve, a hidden oasis of woodland and grassland which includes a wide variety of wildlife and a nature trail. There are over 450 species of plants and it is widely acclaimed for its flora. The reserve is named after the late Dr E.F. Warburg, an Oxford botanist. There is a visitor centre where you can learn more about this fascinating place.

The Walk

From the inn, with the car park opposite, turn right and walk along the lane. After a few yards you reach the spacious grassy expanse of Maidensgrove and Russell's Water Commons. The soil of these commons is owned by the Stonor estate and certain people have registered rights of common. From here are wide views over the wooded Chilterns.

Follow the lane until it bends sharp left towards the houses of Maidensgrove and then turn right to join a waymarked public right of way. The track, known as Hatch Lane, descends towards the dense woods and hidden valleys of the Warburg Nature Reserve. On a sunny day the scene is glorious – a rolling wooded carpet stretching to the horizon. Continue down beside hedgerows, disregarding a path

113

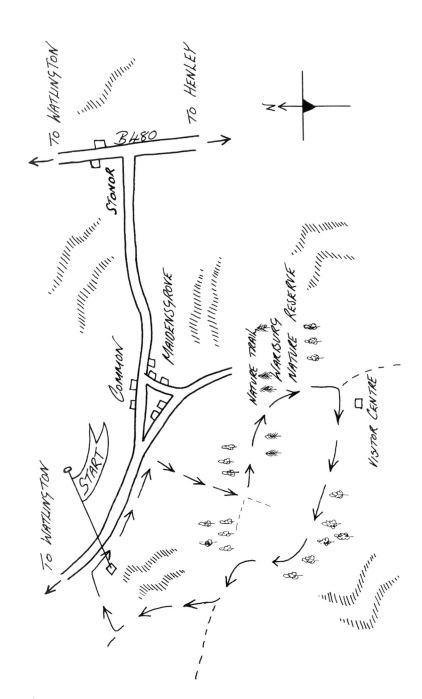

shooting off across the fields on the right.

Further down, amid the trees, bear left at some wooden posts and railings. Follow the Bugle Path, part of the nature trail or wildlife walk, between banks of undergrowth and trees. The path bends left, then right and passes through another wooden barrier. Soon the path graduates to a broad grassy ride running between trees and sunny glades. Along this stretch you may see various spring flowers, including bugle and cowslips. The speckled wood butterfly may be seen here in summer. Information panels provide you with much information about what to see and look for as you progress along the path. Features such as woodland edge management, sheep grazing, coppicing and other aspects concerning the wildlife, history and management of Warburg Reserve are explained in a straightforward way. The reserve lies on either side of a dry winding valley. The pooling of cold air along the valley floor means that there are hard frosts here. Tawny owls are known to breed in these peaceful surroundings, and among the trees to be found in the mixed woodlands are beech, ash, oak, sycamore and lime.

Follow the ride and keep to the path as it veers to the right; when you reach a junction of paths turn left and walk down to the car park near the visitor centre. Go out through the gate and bear right. Follow the track, wet and muddy in places. Pass paths either side of the bridleway and continue. Disregard a track running up the slopes on the right. Along this stretch you may hear, as I did, the distinctive sound of the woodpecker tapping out its nesthole.

Soon the track curves a little to the left and at this point you reach the reserve's boundary. There are now rolling fields either side of you, a fence on the left and a line of trees on the right. At a junction of tracks and paths turn right and follow another muddy track as it cuts through a typical Chiltern landscape characterised by spectacular rolling hills crowned with trees. The track twists and turns and eventually runs along the edge of a beech copse. In damp autumn weather the going on this stretch can often be deceptive; a thick carpet of fallen leaves may conceal deep pockets of mud. Take care!

When the track narrows to a path and plunges into the undergrowth, bear right to cross the fence. There is a white arrow here. Head up the steep slopes of the field, keeping to the edge, and near the top there are magnificent views over the rolling Chilterns and back towards the Warburg Reserve. Pass under some telegraph wires and continue round the top of the field. Look for a wooden stile in the left boundary, cross it and go up the bank to another stile. Continue along the field edge to the next stile. Walk along the field edge of the next field, keeping trees and bushes on your left. At the gate in the corner go out to the road, turn right and return to the inn.

Long Wittenham
The Plough

28

Records indicate that the rambling old Plough inn has been used at various times as a butcher's shop, a slaughterhouse, a dairy and a courtroom for inquests. In the 1900s it was known as the Paraffin Arms due to the method of cooking and heating used. It is understood to have been an inn since the mid 19th century. The history of the Plough is recorded in some detail inside.

The lounge bar has a wood-burning stove, a low-beamed ceiling and several prints of the nearby Thames. You can spend time in the games/ family room, or eat in the restaurant. Starters include soup of the day, prawn cocktail and smoked mackerel. Among the main dishes are 'free-range' sausages – which are a speciality – chicken and ham pie, steak and kidney pie, vegetarian dishes, ploughman's, salmon steak, pizza and curries. Puddings include white ice cream 'bombes', apple strudel and 'death by chocolate'. There is also a traditional Sunday roast.

Beamish is available, as are Fosters and Holstein lagers and Strongbow cider. Real ales include Theakstons, Pedigree and John Smith's Bitter.

The famous throwing game, Aunt Sally, is played in the back garden

which is nearly 300 yards long and runs down to the Thames. The inn has its own moorings; there are also bed and breakfast and camping by permission. Children and dogs are welcome. It is best to book at weekends.
Telephone: 01865 407738.

How to get there: From Abingdon head south-east on the A415. At Clifton Hampden turn right for Long Wittenham. The inn is on the right along the main street.

Parking: There is room to park at the back of the pub. Long Wittenham has a few parking spaces.

Length of the walk: 5 miles. Map: OS Landranger 164 Oxford and surrounding area (GR 546937).

This walk offers a great deal of variety. It begins by following Long Wittenham's long village street and then heads across country to Little Wittenham, a pretty hamlet. If time allows, you can wander down to the Thames at Day's Lock.

The route of the walk leaves the lower ground by making for the Sinodun Hills, or the Wittenham Clumps, as they are more widely known. This is because of the beech trees that crown the hills. The further hill, Castle Hill, includes the earthworks of an Iron Age fort built to defend the nearby river. From the Sinodun Hills there are magnificent views over Oxfordshire and the Thames Valley. The walk returns to Long Wittenham via several roads, tracks and field paths.

The Walk

Leave the pub car park and turn left along Long Wittenham's main street. Pass a turning to the church and continue along the street for a few yards until the road bends left. Veer right at this point and follow the lane towards Little Wittenham. Pass a turning to the Machine Man – an inn. Follow the lane as it cuts through a level landscape of trees and hedgerows. Wittenham Clumps dominate the horizon on this stretch of the walk, clusters of beech trees crowning the distant Sinodun Hills and known throughout Oxfordshire as a popular landmark and local beauty spot.

When the road swings right join a track and head for some farm buildings. On reaching the buildings bear right and then go through some wooden gates. Cross the field by keeping close to the right boundary. Pass into the next field via an old stile and head towards the buildings of Little Wittenham. The wall ahead of you encloses the grounds of a large house in the village. Make for the right-hand end of the wall, cross a stile and walk to the left of some cottages.

Pass a pond and some willow trees and then follow the waymarkers towards the house. The path cuts across the garden – but don't worry, it's a legal right of way. Go across the lawn (there is a tennis court on the right) and then swing right to the white gate in the wall.

Bear left for a few yards; note St Peter's church on the left. Turn right (signposted 'Shillingford Bridge 2 miles'). There is a sign here for Little Wittenham Nature Reserve. The reserve comprises 250 acres of grassland and woodland. Access to the grassland for informal recreation is granted by agreement with Oxfordshire County Council. In front of you there are two paths. Take the right fork and follow the path towards Wittenham Clumps. Go over a stile and then climb the steep grassy slopes towards the trees. At the top of the hill, 393 ft above sea level, there is a magnificent view over an extensive area of Oxfordshire countryside. The Thames is clearly visible upstream at Day's Lock. Over to the west the great chimneys of Didcot Power Station loom into view. From this point, with good visibility it is possible to trace virtually the entire route of this walk.

Pass to the left of the trees and then drop down the slope towards a stile. Castle Hill, dominated by beech trees, stands out clearly ahead of you and is your next objective on the walk. Pass a gate on the left. Cross the stile and then swing right and go up the steps, across the grassy slopes and into the trees. Follow a clear path, turn right after a few yards and emerge from the trees. Descend the bank and swing left towards the car park and the road.

On reaching the road turn right. Follow the lane and shortly you pass the entrance to Hill Farm on the left. There are good views of Wittenham Clumps to the right. Start to descend the slope and then bear left immediately before the Little Wittenham village sign to join a waymarked path. Follow the concrete track to the right of the farm buildings; avoid a turning on the right. Soon the unfenced track becomes grassy; continue to follow it as it curves to the right between barren expanses of fields.

Eventually you reach a stile. Continue ahead keeping to the left boundary of the field. Go through a gate into the next field and keep following the boundary. After several minutes look for a stile in the left-hand hedgerow. Cross it and go out to the road. Turn right and follow the road round the right-hand bend towards Long Wittenham. Take care here as the road can be busy at times. There are good views again on the right over to Wittenham Clumps.

Follow the road as it descends the slope and curves left. Just beyond a field gateway on the right is a narrow opening in the right-hand hedgerow. Drop down to a stile and then cross the field to the far right corner. Negotiate a dilapidated stile and then continue ahead alongside the fields of a pig farm. Follow the track, wide and muddy in places, and when it bends to the left go straight on. Make for the stile in the

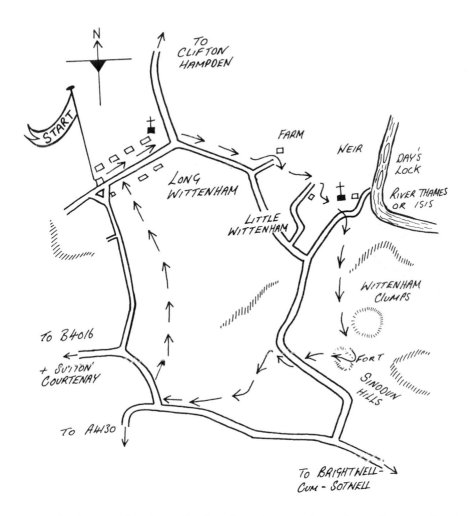

next hedge up ahead. Walk ahead to the next boundary, then across the next field. The route of the path is straight so it is difficult to get lost! In the next boundary there is a stile and a footbridge over a little stream. Continue ahead on a wide path lined by wire fences. Up ahead are the buildings of Long Wittenham.

Glancing back at this stage reveals a splendid view of the tree-smudged Sinodun Hills in the distance. Go through an area of rough grass, wild plants and weeds. When it reaches a track go straight across to join a narrow path running alongside a thatched cottage. At the road turn left and return to the inn.

29 Brightwell Baldwin
The Lord Nelson

The Lord Nelson is very much a restaurant pub and a brasserie, with great emphasis placed on its excellent, inspired menu. Originally a thatched cottage, it was extended in the late 18th century. Not surprisingly, there is a strong nautical theme running through the inn, with various pictures and prints devoted to our great naval traditions. Pictures of famous ships and several ship design plans line the walls. A plaque over the entrance informs you that, having been closed for 66 years, the inn was reopened on 21st October 1971 – Trafalgar Day – by Vice-Admiral Sir William Crawford KBE CB DSC. Inside, there is a splendid inglenook fireplace to warm you after a spell in the fresh air!

Though the menu does not include the more traditional type of pub grub, it does offer something to suit most people's tastes. The inn aims to provide a complete range of meals from bar snacks and light meals to a full à la carte menu. Among the varied starters are home-made soup, duck, liver and port pâté, and warm bacon and mushroom salad and asparagus mousse; among the fish and seafood dishes is lemon sole and among the meat dishes are Cajun spicy chicken salad and pie of the day. There is a selection of salads and snacks, Lord Nelson salad, ploughman's lunch and filled baguettes. On Sunday the restaurant provides a traditional roast. John Smiths, Theakstons, a guest ale, Carlsberg and Kronenbourg lagers and Strongbow draught cider satisfy the thirst.

At the rear is a terrace and a pretty garden with a weeping willow. Children and dogs are welcome. It is also preferable to book, especially for larger groups.

Telephone: 01491 612497.

How to get there: From Watlington follow the B480 towards Chalgrove and turn left at Cuxham for Brightwell Baldwin. The inn is on the left opposite the church.

Parking: There is plenty of room to park at the Lord Nelson, but space is limited in the village itself.

Length of the walk: 3 ½ miles. Map: OS Landranger 164 Oxford and surrounding area (GR 654948).

The walk begins opposite the 14th century church in this peaceful village. Inside are monuments to the Stone family who held the manor here for 400 years. Soon you are crossing Brightwell Park, with its fine cedar trees, and on across rolling farmland dotted with trees and hedgerows to Chalgrove, scene of a famous battle in the Civil War. The return leg of the walk offers glimpses of the spectacular Chiltern Hills.

The Walk

Emerging from the inn, turn right and walk along the road. Pass Brightwell Baldwin Cottage and Glebe Barn. Bear left at the way-marker post (Chalgrove 1 ¾ miles). Enter the refined grounds of Brightwell Park. Aim slightly left across the parkland, passing between ancient cedar trees. Look for a gate in the far boundary; as you head towards it, there are good views of the Georgian stable block over to the left. The original late 18th century house has gone but the stable block has been converted into a private residence. There is also a 17th century dovecote designed in the shape of a Greek cross.

Go through the wooden kissing-gate   look out for the huge cedar tree with its great solid trunk shaped and weathered by the centuries – and follow a straight path towards a white gate. Go through a wrought-iron gate and continue ahead to the next gate. Pass through the gate and follow a wide grassy path between trees and scrub. After several hundred yards you reach a stile on the edge of a field. Bear left

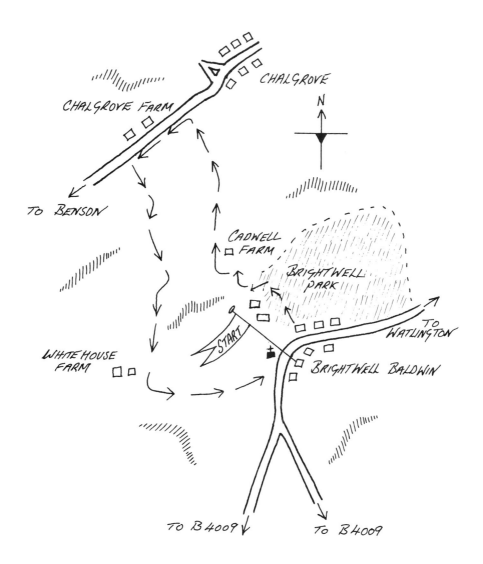

CHALGROVE FARM

CHALGROVE

N

TO BENSON

CADWELL FARM

BRIGHTWELL PARK

START

TO WATLINGTON

WHITE HOUSE FARM

BRIGHTWELL BALDWIN

TO B4009

TO B4009

and follow the clear track round the perimeter of the field. There is woodland on the left. In the field corner turn right and skirt the southern boundary of the field.

Soon the rough surface of the track shifts to concrete. Follow the track round to the left and head towards the buildings of Cadwell Farm. Just beyond the bend is a seat in memory of the President of the Chalgrove branch of the Royal British Legion. All around you at this stage of the walk are views over gently rolling, semi-wooded countryside.

Follow the track alongside the farm buildings and continue beyond a turning on the left ('private – no footpath'). Pass a public footpath on the right and head towards the edge of some light woodland and undergrowth. There are lines of pine trees here. Soon the track breaks cover from the trees and rises gently between fields. The church tower at Chalgrove edges into view at this point. Continue on the track and pass a sign 'Game preserved – please keep dogs under control'.

Soon you reach the road. If time allows, you may want to look round Chalgrove. The village is famous for the Battle of Chalgrove Field during the Civil War. A stone memorial was erected here in 1843 on the two-hundredth anniversary of Colonel John Hampden's death. Hampden, a leading Parliamentarian and MP, was vigorously opposed to Charles I's Ship Tax and this was one of the crucial factors which sparked off the Civil War. Hampden was fatally wounded in battle and died at nearby Thame, his way blocked by Royalist troops. Prince Rupert successfully fought the Parliamentary force on the 'fair plain called Chalgrove Field' and then travelled on victorious to Oxford with almost 200 prisoners he had taken at Chalgrove.

Return to the junction with the track and continue along the lane; pass some tall conifer hedging enclosing several properties and then the entrance to Chalgrove Farm. Several hundred yards beyond the gate is a waymarked path on the left (Ewelme 3 miles). Take the path, muddy in places, and follow it between fields. The wooded escarpment of the Chilterns is visible a little to the left. At the field corner veer slightly right and follow a muddy, well-used path to reach the corner of some woodland. Skirt the field edge, with the trees on the right. At the next corner, where a track crosses our route, go straight ahead for a few yards into the field in front of you. Veer right for a short distance and then bear left on to a waymarked path running up the middle of the field towards Whitehouse Farm. Further up, the path runs alongside crops before reaching the farm buildings. Follow the path along the left-hand side of the farm and when you draw level with the house, where the drive swings away to the left, go straight ahead across the lawn towards a gap in the woodland.

Follow the track through a tunnel of trees and when it bends right go straight ahead for a few yards to join a firm track which veers left. (The path to Ewelme is straight on.) Keep to the track as it cuts across the fields; the tree-clad Chilterns are clearly visible now. The track eventually bends right at some double gates. At this point swing half-left to join a bridleway. Follow it with a field on the left and trees and hedgerow on the right. Soon a gate takes you into the next field; continue ahead with a fence on the right. Shortly the trees give way to reveal splendid views of the Chiltern ridge. Ahead of you are the trees and rooftops of Brightwell Baldwin. In the field corner go through a gate and join a track running down between fences. The bridleway can be very wet and muddy in places.

At the road, opposite Brightwell Park, turn right and pass Meadow Cottage. At the junction bear sharp left and return to the village centre. There is a good view of Brightwell Park through the gateway on the left.

30 Cuxham
The Half Moon

The Half Moon is one of Cuxham's most picturesque buildings. Recorded as a 'shoppe and butterie' in 1662 and distinguished by its charming thatched roof, the inn boasts a bar, eating area and family room, as well as some distinctive features, including 3 open fires, a beamed ceiling, a French dresser and an antique Singer sewing machine. The church brass at Cuxham is inscribed with the coat of arms of the Gregory family and the design contains a half moon, which may have provided the inspiration for the inn's name.

Food is served every day except Sunday evening. There is a daily specials board and a range of bar snacks – jacket potatoes, baguettes, ploughman's and salads among them. For something more substantial, there is a wide selection of starters and an extensive choice of main courses, including sirloin steak, English lamb cutlets, gammon steak, wholetail scampi, swordfish of tuna steak, garlic and herb chicken, home-made seafood pie, chicken balti and chilli and potato wedges. The inn is also renowned for its pies – game pie, lamb pie and steak and Brakspear pie. On Sunday there is a traditional roast, as well as a good selection of starters and other dishes. The Half Moon also offers a children's menu, as well as cream teas in summer – an ideal way to round off an afternoon walk in the countryside. Brakspear Old Ale and Bitter are among the beers; there is also Strongbow draught cider and

Guinness, and Stella Artois and Heineken for the lager drinker.

At the rear of the pub is a delightful garden partly sheltered by the branches of an oak tree and overlooking fields and downland beyond. The garden includes a children's play area and in summer the landlord holds barbecues. Dogs preferably outside.

Telephone: 01491 614110.

How to get there: From Watlington take the B480 towards Chalgrove and Stadhampton. Follow the road into Cuxham and the inn is in the main street.

Parking: The Half Moon has its own car park. Alternatively, there are a few spaces elsewhere in the village.

Length of the walk: 3¼ miles. Map: OS Landranger 164 Oxford and surrounding area (GR 667954).

Cuxham occupies a pleasant rural setting and in this area are springs which rise beneath the nearby Chilterns. The walk cuts across country to the village of Pyrton, providing good views over these hills. The scenery on this route may not be as spectacular as that offered by nearby Watlington Hill, but it is a remote hidden expanse of countryside where you are unlikely to encounter many other people. Ideal for those wanting to escape 'the madding crowd.'

The Walk

From the inn turn left and walk along the B480 road until you reach a lay-by and a bridleway (signposted Pyrton Heath House) on the left. Take the bridleway, go up the hill and when the track levels out, there are wide views over an extensive area of Oxfordshire; the wooded Chilterns can easily be seen from here. Soon the track bends right; keep on it with a hedgerow on your left now. The sign for Pyrton Heath House comes into view shortly and at this point you veer right by a hard tennis court to join a waymarked bridleway. After a few yards the way bends left by some children's swings. The main house can be seen over to the left.

Follow the edge of the grounds and continue ahead on the grassy path away from the house. Maintain the same direction for some time and head towards some woodland in the distance. Pass a 'private' track running off to the right. Look out for a seat at the side of the woodland; in the corner of the field turn right by a blue waymark and now the walk coincides with the route of the Oxfordshire Way. Aim for a line of trees with the ridge of the Chilterns forming the distant backdrop. Pass the strip of woodland and enter the next field by continuing to follow

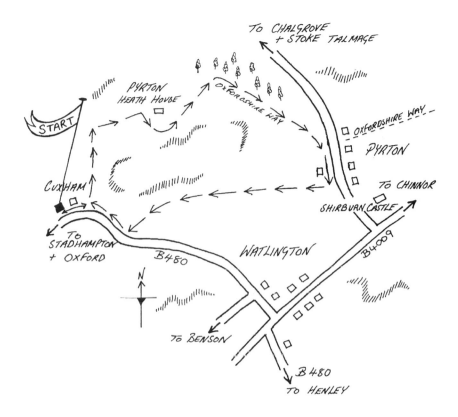

the track. This is a particularly isolated tract of countryside where dense woodland cuts you off from civilisation and the only signs of life may be animal rather than human.

Pass another line of trees on the right and then a 'private' track. Walk along the track as it skirts the right-hand edge of the field, pass a bungalow and then emerge at the road. Turn right and pass a thatched cottage. This was once a pub; now only the inn sign remains. Opposite the cottage are the grounds of moated Shirburn Castle, hidden by walls and trees. In the 18th century it belonged to Thomas Parker who was Lord Chancellor and Earl of Macclesfield under George I. The 'silver-tongued Parker' was charged with corruption and retired to Shirburn in disgrace. He died in 1732. The manor house belonged to the Symeon family whose daughter married John Hampden in the early 17th century. Hampden fought and died in the Civil War Battle of Chalgrove Field.

Take the waymarked path on the right (signposted to Cuxham) and follow it along the edge of a private garden. In the corner, by a tool shed, go over a stile and into a paddock. Follow the left boundary and cross the stile in the corner. Veer half-right across the grass, cross a track leading to some barns and outbuildings and go over a stile into another paddock. Cross the field diagonally to a gate on the far side; cross a stream and then bear right in the field. Follow the perimeter and keep the stream over to your right. Eventually you reach the field corner – there is a copse in front of you now. Turn right and pass over the stream into the adjacent field. Bear left to a gate. Go through it and then walk ahead along the left-hand boundary. There is woodland over on the right.

Cross into the next field and continue along its boundary with a ditch and a line of trees on your immediate left. Also over to the left is the outline of the glorious Chiltern hills. After some time you reach the field corner. Exit from the field at this point and walk round beside some hay barns and cottages to the B480 road. Turn right and pass Chestnut Farm Cottages. After a few yards the road curves left to reach the lay-by encountered at the start of the walk. Continue along the road and very soon you are back at the Half Moon in Cuxham.